S0-BKF-009

ART—
WR

1 2 3
Be a
PORN ST★R!

ALSO BY ANA LORIA

*GET PAID FOR SEX! The Big Bad Book of Sex
Opportunities for Men and Women*
(*INFONET PUBLICATIONS, 1999*)

1 2 3
Be a
PORN ST★R!

Ana Loria

**A step-by-step guide to the adult sex industry
FOR MEN AND WOMEN**

INFONET PUBLICATIONS
MALIBU, CALIFORNIA

3 1336 05559 6705

Copyright © 2000 by INFONET PUBLICATIONS

All rights reserved. Manufactured and printed in the United States of America by INFONET PUBLICATIONS. No part of this book may be reproduced or transmitted in any form or by any means, electronic or mechanical, including photo copying, recording, or by information storage and retrieval system, or for any reason, without the written permission of the publisher, except for inclusions of brief quotations in review.

ISBN: 0-9651190-2-5
First Edition, Printed January 2000

Cover design by Clive Young.
Photographs of Ana Loria, Mariah Wind, Bill Margold, and Jim South by InfoNet Publications.

Grateful acknowledgment is made to the following for permission to reprint:

Adam & Eve (photos of Nina Hartley)
Astral Ocean (photo of Jill Kelly)
Filmwest Productions (photo of Max Hardcore and Julianna Sterling)
Five K Sales (photo of Sharon Mitchell)
John T-Bone Studios (photo of Annabel Chong)
Guy DeSilva (photo of Guy DeSilva)
VCA Pictures (photos of Ashlyn Gere and Randy West)
Vidco Entertainment (photo of Peter North)

This publication is intended for general informational purposes only, and it should not be construed as legal advice, considered applicable, or be relied upon in any specific circumstances. Readers seeking legal advice should engage a licensed attorney. Any references to companies, products or services are purely illustrative and do not constitute an endorsement. Neither the publisher nor the author advocate that the reader violate any laws concerning indecency or sexual activity. While every effort has been made to ensure the reliability of the information in this publication, InfoNet Publications does not guarantee the accuracy of the data presented. Errors brought to the attention of the publisher will be corrected in future editions.

Discounts are available on this book for bulk purchases.
To order additional copies or to learn about other books
by the publisher, please contact:

INFONET PUBLICATIONS
23852 Pacific Coast Highway, PMB 330
Malibu, California, USA 90265-4879
(310) 388-1026
www.dirtybooks.com

For everyone who loves sex and hates violence

Table of Contents

Acknowledgments

I'd like to humbly thank everyone who helped in researching and writing this book: Annabel Chong, Guy DeSilva, Luke Ford, Ashlyn Gere, Max Hardcore, Nina Hartley, David Heller, Lise Hilboldt, Jill Kelly, Mr. Marcus, Bill Margold, Sharon Mitchell and her staff at AIM Health Care Foundation, Peter North, Henri Pachard, Sean Rich, Gary Sage, Jim South and his staff at World Modeling Agency, Stephanie Swift, Stacy Valentine, Randy West, Mariah Wind, and Clive Young.

My conversations and interactions with these people—as well as many others in the business—has taught me an important lesson. Workers in the adult industry continue to be stigmatized and criticized, while they are in fact some of the most ethical, loyal, and friendly people I have ever met. We owe them all a debt of gratitude for working daily to expand our appreciation of sexuality and its beauty

Also, undying thanks to my research assistant M.C.D., for all his valuable hard work and dutiful assistance. (Of course, he got to meet some of the porn stars, so maybe it wasn't *that* difficult.) And a very special thanks and love to my proofreader and copy editor L.M.S., for having what a great American writer once called "a built-in bullshit detector."

Most of all, I'd like to dedicate this book to all of the people of adult cinema who are no longer with us—your films and legends are there forever to remind people of the hurdles you had to endure to help make the business of X what it is today: a legitimate form of artistic expression and commercial enterprise.

Introduction

Being a renowned safe-sex maven and titillating webmistress, I recently visited the VSDA (Video Software Dealers Association) Expo in Los Angeles. Quite simply, I was brought to my knees by the crowds of people who showed up to see the porn stars and find out about all the ways one can profit from the adult sex industry in the 21st century. I spent the day traversing the Expo, asking questions and hanging out with all my friends and acquaintances. Later, when I returned to my Malibu beach house, I realized that I had collected quite a lot of notes and interviews with some of the tried and true of the "X Business." After reading through them, your humble lil' lovette came to an important realization: *there has never been a better time to be a professional flesh muffin—male or female.*

I decided right then to chronicle once and for all, and with no bull-shit, how anyone with a powerful libido and a desire to meet interesting people can enjoy a satisfying career in the adult industry. What follows is a guide that can fit right in your back pocket (and won't fall out when your Leading Lord or Lady rips your pants off) packed full of up-to-date information one can't find in the local library. You will learn who the right people are, what they do, and how you can meet them. You'll learn practical details about producers, agents, directors, distributors, financial matters, resources, contracts, auditions, organizations and health concerns. Best of all, you will hear direct, exclusive quotes from porn legends who will guide you through the pitfalls of this competitive industry. And, who knows? Maybe you might decide that this type of work is for you.

'Nuff said. Now, let's get to the sex!

—Ana Loria
Malibu, CA

1

The Stuff

(AS IN: "DO YOU HAVE IT?")

"Sex has been around a long, long time... I don't see it going away."
—*David F. Friedman, adult film pioneer*

We live in a country that is the world's leading producer of porn, churning out a mind-blowing 10,000 titles a year. In comparison, Hollywood only puts out about 400 theatrical films a year. This means that if Blockbuster Video carried X-rated films, you'd find 150 new adult titles on the shelves every week! In other words, the adult industry is as American as apple pie, and it makes perfect sense if you think about it. Porn has not only led to landmark court decisions, but it has also trail-blazed numerous cutting-edge media technologies. Not that porn has always gotten the credit for doing such things—the industry still remains a sort of moral outcast and target for conservative tight-asses. Let's face it, America will never NOT be uptight about making love.

But you've heard the expression "money talks, bullshit walks"? Well, the porn industry has spoken loudest in how much cash it generates: $10 billion a year from video, cable, hotels, Digital/DVD, mail-order, Internet, CD-ROM and phone sex services. According to journalist Luke Ford in *The History of X*: "Americans now spend more money at strip clubs than at plays, opera, ballet, and music combined."

As I stood in line at the VSDA Convention to get my press credentials, I met a man who had spent the last 30 years building casinos. "I'm here because I'm looking into investing in adult film," he told me. "This business is growing so fast that in a few years the amount of money to be made off porn is going to dwarf the casino industry." When I asked him if he would ever consider being a performer, he blushed and said, "Well, I don't think so, but you never know. That might be an added perk of being the money man."

The following chapter is actually less about the "money men" than about the real backbone of the adult film industry: the legions of adult performers who work their cute, tight butts and bodies off in front of the camera. After reading about their experiences, you will be better prepared to decide whether you are ready to step up to bat, so to speak. Remember, the more you know *before* you set foot in an agent's office, the easier it will be to launch a successful career in the world of porn.

A. QUESTIONS TO ASK

1. "Why Do I Want To Do This?"

This can be the hardest question to answer, but it's probably also the most important. People get into porn for as many reasons as there are ears in a cornfield: lust, loneliness, money, rebellion—you name it. According to porn veteran and talent counselor Bill Margold, the common denominator is one's ego. "If you are entering porn because you want to be famous, you are in luck," he tells potential Leading Lords and Ladies. "If you're into the glory and will go to the ends of the earth to satisfy that lust, at least egotistically, you have what it takes to be a porn star." However, there are right and wrong reasons for getting into porn, just as there are right and wrong reasons for entering any money-making venture.

Money. One of the biggest draws to porn is that it offers a unique package of part-time work for full-time pay. If you save your money, invest it wisely and live modestly, you can work three days a week and still make enough to be comfortable. Then, you can use the extra time to go to school, learn a trade, or pursue that creative writing or underwater basket-weaving career.

Let us put one thing to rest, though. If all you are interested in is money, go be a day trader. Honestly, there are easier ways of making cash. Not that the fast money can't help you make some ends meet. But if you want to be consistently employed by directors or producers, your "just-for-the-money" attitude will show through in your performances and hurt your chances of having an even bigger and better career.

If the money still draws you despite what I've said, keep in mind that by appearing in porn films you might make a lot of money one week and very little the next. Porn people who aren't used to money or don't know how to handle it often blow their earnings quickly. I advise you to consider getting a respectable accountant to help you manage your affairs and keep you out of harm's way of scammers or the IRS.

Fame. The second biggie. Fame is undoubtedly a tantalizing prospect for anyone who dances naked in front of their bedroom mirror to the applause of an imaginary audience. Yes, fame is definitely a perk of being a porn star—but what kind of fame is it? There are a lot of smart men and women in porn, but there are also a lot of starstruck people who think that this is going to be their way to easy street. "If you play your cards right, there can be a certain amount of fame and money," says Gary Sage, winner of the coveted *Hot D'or '99* for Best New American Porn Director, "but it's one of those situations where you have to be careful what you ask for; you might not want that type of fame." You may get off the bus from Ohio, make four or five movies in a week, earn a couple grand, go home and forget about it. Then, six or eight months down the line your friend's great-grandfather will see you on a hotel pay-per-view channel!

"This is not Hollywood," porn legend Nina Hartley told me. "This is not like any other business. This is sex on camera for forever. You may leave in six months and become a born-again Christian. The image is out there forever. Someone will come up to you in ten years and go, 'Is this you?' Once you've made the commitment to be on camera having sex, you have to believe and understand that it's not going to go away no matter what you do. It could come back to haunt you."

Porn legend and sex-positivist Nina Hartley looking great as usual.

Making a Statement. You may be at heart a rebellious outlaw who enjoys shocking the uptight world from whence you came. Truth is, porn was much more powerful as a social or political statement back in its early days, when it was seen as an offshoot of the sexually adventurous 60s and 70s. (It was also illegal!) In 1986, Bill Margold sat before the Meese Commission on Pornography and told them: "In a society that is drug-infested, violence-wracked, and polluted by chemical greed, no one's ever died from an overdose of pornography." Nina Hartley, who describes herself as a "bisexual feminist exhibitionist," entered porn largely to express and advance her own personal beliefs about sex. (Both were arrested in Las Vegas in 1993 as part of the scandalous 'Erotic Eleven.') Nowadays, you will find that the World of X has advanced to more of a established business. Hardly anybody enters it as a political statement anymore, although many porn moguls are still politically active. Director John "Buttman" Stagliano, for example, is a regular contributor to the Cato Institute, a liberal Washington think tank, where he often discusses policy issues with its economists!

A newer porn star who uses her sex as a statement is Annabel Chong, a journalism student at USC who broke into the business working with John T. Bone on 1997's *The World's Biggest Gang Bang*. Fascinated with sex from more than just a physical standpoint, Annabel recently made her own documentary on sex in American society. She was also the subject of the controversial 1998 documentary *Sex: The Annabel Chong Story*, which played to standing-room-only crowds at the Sundance Film Festival.

Exhibitionism. This is arguably the defining characteristic of most of the men and women in the Land of X. You are either born with the desire for attention or you aren't. It's something that can't really be taught. All the great performers—from Ron Jeremy to John Leslie; Marilyn Chambers to Ashlyn Gere; Georgina Spelvin to Vanessa Del Rio; Jamie Gillis to Rocco Siffredi—have had this characteristic, which results in their very different but very memorable performances. Out of this sense of exhibitionism comes what Bill Margold calls "the two best reasons for getting into porn: notoriety and immortality." Appearing in porn films will offer you plenty of both. If you truly enjoy the performance aspect of sex, such that you feed off the exhibitionist thrill, then porn is likely the right industry for you.

Pure Lust. Ahhh, I couldn't wait to get to this section, because, your humble lil' sex mistress can personally identify with this emotion. Lust is a very powerful thing in America—one that is dealt with equal parts pride and shame. Male or female, you should have very little of the latter. "Most women in the industry say they enjoy the sex, some more so, some less," wrote *GQ* magazine. "But they all agree you have to like it a little or you'll lose your mind. You show up for work, and you just let yourself get carried away; you fall in love with your scene partner for as long as it takes for the film to get shot. Then you go back home. It's like getting paid for a one-day affair."

Men can probably afford to be a little more detached about their performances, yet they must be lusty enough to hold an erection for up to two hours at a time under the most difficult of circumstances. While 98.9% of the male population on earth loves sex, a true woodsman has to *crave* it. Bobby Vitale started out as a happily married man who detailed cars for a living. The problem was that he was horny all the time. After a year of begging and pleading, a production company finally gave him a chance. Now he's one of only three male adult performers signed to an exclusive contract with porn biggie Vivid, and recently he appeared in a film entitled *The Luckiest Man in the World*, where he boned 101 women on a tennis court at high noon. Hard cock to hard cash—not bad!

The Swinging Lifestyle. Many porn stars—Nici Sterling, Nina Hartley, Rayenne, Kaitlyn Ashley—got actively involved in porn as an extension of their desire for sexual experimentation outside their marriages. (In fact, the subculture of swingers is how many people, especially those in Southern California, make contacts with those in the business.) Popular couples, married or not, have included Blondi Bee & Tony Montana, Misty Rain & Chad Thomas, Racquel Darrian & Micky Ray, Candida Royale & Per Sjostedt, Tabitha & Jake Steed and Danielle Rogers & Randy Spears. This has its advantages, as a husband-and-wife team or a regular couple has a better chance of getting into the Industry by performing together, and many of the big directors like Bruce Seven and Patrick Collins often direct their own spouses. Make sure you discuss this between yourselves to see if this is something you both want to do. There's a big difference between performing for your camcorder and doing each other on camera in front of an entire crew.

Once you've thought it over and discussed it, you might even find it beneficial to go in together. Porn star Missy was slightly uncomfortable when she entered the porn scene. When her husband started doing it, she became less anxious. Husbands should remember though, that often it is the woman, if she gets a shot on camera, who has to request her spouse, just like she would request any leading woodsman. The man also has to be able to handle the fact that his girl will have sex with other male performers. (Sometimes, the boyfriend isn't even allowed on the set until the third or fourth shoot.) Remember, this probably won't be the most intimate sex you have. This is sex on-camera for money. Both of you have to be emotionally ready to handle that, and it's not everyone who can. "In this business," Bill Margold likes to say, "sex is like shaking hands. It shouldn't be taken too seriously."

A Backdoor into Show Business? Hmm, maybe I should have put this first on the list, since doing porn often gets people further away from their mainstream goal than closer to it. Things have been changing, although slowly. Thanks in part to mainstream films like *The People vs. Larry Flynt* and *Boogie Nights*, which romanticized porn's 1977-1984 'Golden Age' and featured cameos by porn legends Nina Hartley and Veronica Hart, the World of X has been rather hot 'n' hip lately.

In fact, porn has been going mainstream in a huge way. Superstarlet Jenna Jameson recently appeared in Howard Stern's hit movie *Private Parts* and now manages for the World Wrestling Federation. Stern himself has featured porn stars like Houston, Janine, Christie Lake, Kendra Jade, Lisa Lennox and Jill Kelly on his radio and TV shows. VCA contract girl Juli Ashton is the host of The Playboy Channel's *Night Calls*, the spokes-woman for 3 or 4 different dildo companies, and she had the notable honor of being the first porn star to be featured in *Playboy* magazine. Ashlyn Gere, one of the few porn actresses to have a coveted Screen Actors' Guild (SAG) card, has appeared on the hit TV show *The X-Files*. Starlets such as Jenteal hawk products like Swatch, Fresh Jive skatewear, Black Fly sunglasses, Warp snowboards, Van's sneakers and Hard Candy cosmetics (which actually has a fragrance called 'Porno'!). Ron Jeremy popped up in the films *The Chase*, *Killing Zoe* and 1998's *Orgazmo*. Porn starlets frequently appear in MTV videos by Everclear and Metallica. They also date rock stars and often pop up on their albums. Vivid's Dyanna Lauren and Kobe Tai sang backup on Marilyn Manson's *Mechanical Animals*; Houston, Coral Sands, and Claudia Chase posed in a bubble-bath with Kid Rock on the vinyl version of his smash *Devil Without A Cause*; Janine appeared in nurse's uniform and rubber glove on the cover of Blink 182's *Enema of the State*. The porn-rock crossover seemed complete when Sugar Ray's Mark McGrath and Limp Bizkit's Fred Durst appeared in Matt Zane's *Backstage Sluts 2*, in which they regaled viewers with tales of group-sex with groupies.

Still, in thirty years of porn, only two starlets have achieved major mainstream attention. Marilyn Chambers, star of 1973's *Behind The Green Door,* starred in David Cronenberg's horror film *Rabid*, but she was already semi-famous as the *Ivory Snow* girl. Traci Lords, even though she is loathed by the Industry for lying about her age when she started doing porn films, has sung on albums by the Manic Street Preachers and the Ramones and even recorded her own techno-dance album. Traci has also appeared in B-movies like *Not of this Earth*, *Blood Money* and *Skinner* and on TV pro-grams like *Roseanne* and *Melrose Place*. Her biggest achievement was her role in John Waters' *Cry-Baby*.

Unfortunately, those who get in Hollywood's door are often typecast because of their sex work: Ginger Lynn, Vivid's first contract superstar, appeared in some particularly cheesy movies when she left the adult indus-try. In fact, Ginger's non-sex movies don't sound that different from her porn ones: *Bound and Gagged*, *I Was a Teeenage Sex Mutant* and *Vice Academy*.

Even when she landed a small role in *NYPD Blue*, she played a hooker. Jerry Butler, often considered the best actor ever in X, turned down a role on ABC's hit sitcom *Three's Company* because they wanted him to play a porn star.

2. "Is This The Right Line Of Work For Me?"

This issue is quite simple. First, ask yourself: "Is sex my calling?" It's one thing to be horny, but to be horny to the point where you can fuck in front of a festival crowd is another thing again. Your own beliefs are important, as is the reaction you will have to yourself for doing this work. Next ask yourself tough questions like "Am I okay with what I'm doing?" and "Am I content with the choice I've made?" You will be having sex for a living—it's important that you don't deny or underplay this fact. The more level-headed you are about yourself, the better off you'll be. It really depends on who you are, what your look is, and what you want, whether you want to make it your life. "And it will be your life," says director Gary Sage. "You don't go home at 5pm and say hello to your neighbors and go out with your bowling league. Once you're a porno star it does become your life. It's like being a celebrity. If you have a problem with this then you shouldn't do it."

Nina Hartley offers a valuable home quiz to test your performing potential. "This is how you can know if you can work in porn. Gather 15 friends, get naked in front of them, and masturbate to orgasm. If you can handle that, you're in."

3. "What Do I Hope To Gain?"

Short-term vs. Long-term. This is connected to your reasons for wanting to pursue a career in porn. Maybe you're sick of your crappy waitering job, and you just need some temporary extra cash. Or maybe you are planning to build yourself a small sex empire. This is something you might try to work out before you film your first scene. The benefits of short-term porn work mean that, among other things, you can make quick money, you won't get drawn so completely into the industry (although your movies will be on the shelves forever and ever and ever…) and, quite simply, you won't get sick of sex.

Many porn stars, especially the women, are known for spending all the money they make in films. (Or they get into sex flicks to pay off already accumulated massive debt.) Thus, short-term careers become long-term careers not by choice but because the star is always behind. For every one porn star who jumps in and jumps out in order to pursue an outside goal—the very popular Nikki Dial was only in the business about a year before she left with enough funds to go to law school—there are tons who continually plan to get out *after* their next gig. Staying in too long can mess with a head that's not prepared to handle it: the much-publicized suicides of starlets Shauna Grant ('84), Alex Jordan ('95) and Savannah ('94) have been attributed to people who stayed in the business too long for the wrong, if differently wrong, reasons.

Opinions of those in the business vary widely on how long one should stick with it, even among respected actresses/producers/directors like Sarah Jane Hamilton (a.k.a. Veronica Hart). She once claimed that everyone should eventually wean themselves off the industry. Of course, Ms. Hamilton's been in porn for 18 years—so go figure.

B. ISSUES TO CONSIDER

1. Social Stigma

Now more than ever would seem the right time to enter the jizz biz. Unfortunately, this is America, and being a place that was founded by Pilgrims and Puritans, it's still kinda "funny" about sex. Pornography continues to be the most convenient scapegoat for every social ill from AIDS to The Mafia to bad breath. According to Brit journalist Laurence O'Toole, it's part of a grand American tradition of searching for the "enemy within—whether it is Communists, gays, immigrants, single mothers, UFOs or porn." Porn stars, porn sets, porn producers, porn directors, porn distributors, porn retailers (and even porn connoisseurs) have all been busted countless times over the years by the police and by the government ever since the 1920s and the era of back-room stag films. In the 1980s, when the Reagan-appointed Meese Commission condemned the industry and the FBI launched its notorious "MIPORN' investigations, it got really bad: the staff of a chain of eight adult video stores in Dallas were arrested 1,250 times!

How does this personally affect the average adult industry performer? On a very general level, porn stars tend to be misunderstood by society. For instance, Nina Hartley has encountered many anti-porn feminists who accuse her of not being aware that she is being "exploited" or "mistreated." The scene in *Boogie Nights* where porn star Amber Waves (Julianne Moore) fights a losing battle with her ex-husband to win custody of her child is actually an accurate assessment of the stigma still attached to being in X. When veteran actress and activist Sharon Mitchell counsels those wishing to enter the word of porn, she tells them: "If you have children and are in a custody battle, you will lose your children." Again, you will achieve a certain kind of fame—but it might not be the kind you wanted or even expected. You are a public image when you appear in porn. You have crossed that social line and to a certain extent, you don't have control over that. It can play head games on those who, blinded by dollar signs and flashing light bulbs, haven't sincerely thought about what they're getting into.

This is why porn performers develop strong bonds with each other. The camaraderie comes from what the people in it already bring to the industry before they ever get on the set. Virtually all of them are rebels at heart who are involved in porn almost in spite of their roots. David Friedman, director of some of the first sexually explicit films of the 50s, had a father who edited the conservative paper *Birmingham News*. Porn maverick John "Buttman" Stagliano, one of the most respected filmmakers in the business, grew up in a strict conservative household. Porn legend Rhonda Jo Petty was a Mormon from Utah, one of the few "anti-X" states left in the U.S. One of porn's biggest rebels—as well as biggest scandals—was Missy Manners, star of *Behind the Green Door: The Sequel* (1986): as Elisa Flores, she was a former aide to conservative Republican senator Orrin Hatch. (You go, girl!)

2. Personal Relationships

Of course, being an 'outlaw' has its drawbacks. The prime example of this is in the personal relationships (i.e., family, friends, spouses, lovers) that porn stars carry on while they work in the business. Just like the regular film industry, people meet, make friends and connections, date, fall in love and marry. But to be honest, it ain't easy. This is a business where you will often have sex with people five minutes after you first meet them. The nature of the business almost encourages it. And more often than not, the steamiest sex scenes are with people you don't know.

Friendship. Like regular Hollywood stars, adult industry stars have a specific lifestyle associated with life in show business: personal appearances, signings, movies, interviews, etc. Like being a celebrity, porn stars end up befriending and even dating those within the industry—it just happens that way because of the busy work schedules that keep porn stars in sort of an extended family. The unique experience of being a porn star is where some of the strongest bonds can happen. Porn veteran Sharon Mitchell describes her 25-year plus friendship with Nina Hartley as one with a singular sort of bond: "[Nina and I] both danced on the same circuit and in the same clubs for years; finally, we traded stories—one of which is when you are dancing sometimes your costume gets in the way of you needing to pee, so sometimes I'd sort of slip outside, pull aside my contraption down there, and pee in the dumpster. It was only until years later that we found out we peed in some of the same dumpsters." She laughs. "Now that's a fuckin' bond!"

Family. Paul ("PT") Thomas, arguably modern porn's most successful director, told *Premiere* magazine that one of the few accurate things about *Boogie Nights*'s depiction of porn's 'Golden Age' was that the World of X is like an extended family. You fuck together (on and off camera), sit around bored on a set together, endure the same politics of the industry—it's natural that the precious few who know what it's like to work in X would become a protective and oftentimes defensive extended family unit. Bill Margold, who started the porn-star counseling service Protecting Adult Welfare (P.A.W.), has been in the adult business for over 30 years. (See the Appendix for contact information on P.A.W.) As a self-appointed "father" of the Industry, he literally calls all of the young actors and actresses he advises "kids." His apartment in West Hollywood and P.AW.'s office are like demilitarized zones where abused or troubled talent can come and pour out their problems—Bill owns over 1,000 teddy bears. Nina Hartley and Sharon Mitchell are sort of the blonde and brunette versions of "Mom." They too counsel young men and ladies on avoiding the pitfalls (and emotional dumpsters) that they survived to tell about. Like a family, porn stars argue with each other, annoy each other, play politics with each other, stab each other in the back and stand up for each other. "Porn can be a very accepting environment," Nina Hartley explained to me at the VSDA Expo. "It's a much more nurturing environment than what I call the 'real' or 'legitimate' world." This is true mainly because the people who gravitate towards working in porn already feel "different" from normal society because of their unusual, radical, or intense sexual natures. Such people come to porn in search of the non-judgmental atmosphere it provides. To paraphrase that ol' saying, "The Family That Lays Together Stays Together."

Your real family is something else again. Many porn stars won't even tell their families—why do you think even the camera crews in porn use fake names? Countless porn stars have found themselves estranged from their loved ones. The porn legend Marilyn Chambers admitted that both her parents stopped speaking to her for years. Nina Hartley's brother only recently began speaking to her—after 13 years. The thing to note about these people is that they didn't stop doing porn despite what their families said. Jill Kelly, porn's newest superstar, concedes "mom and dad would like to see me do something else for a living, but they've come to terms with it and are supportive of what I do—especially since I've been very responsible with my success." Jill's mom actually prepares, packages and ships Jill's costumes to her for magazine layouts and photo shoots!

Lovers and Spouses. Understandably, this is the most complex part of being in the porn business. How would you feel if your sweetie was being DP'ed by two well-oiled studs? How would you like seeing your man's mansword being swabbed with the saliva of two hot babes? It really comes down to your belief system and how comfortable you, or both of you, feel about what you do for a living. "You are performing the act of intimacy without the intimacy," says Sharon Mitchell.

Opinions vary on the average success or failure of the relationships of people in the porn business. Even those who actively pursue porn stars in relationships, like movie or rock stars, often don't stick around for long. At the top of her fame, starlet Savannah dated comedian Pauly Shore and musicians Vince Neil, Billy Idol, Slash, and "Marky Mark" Wahlberg—years before he would play Dirk Diggler in *Boogie Nights*. Many, except for Slash, wanted her to get out of X-rated films. (Their lifestyles could continue, by the way.) All, including Slash, eventually dumped her.

Porn can bring a lot of stress into a relationship, especially if one of the partners is not in porn. There are a lot of 'What ifs?' in these situations: "What is she doing at work *right now*? Is he going to run into someone who is more exciting than me? Will she make a film with someone who can please her better than me? Does he have a bigger cock than I do?" etc. On the other hand, if both partners are in the business, it can be equally difficult. For instance, men tend to work a lot more for a lot less money, which can lead to conflict and jealousy within the relationship. Couples should remember that doing it onscreen with each other is emotionally different than doing it at home.

Probably the cautionary tale for all couples in the World of X is that of Jill Kelly and her husband Cal Jammer—a story that maps out all the complexities that can occur between males and females in X. Jill had met Cal when she was first starting to do porn. They were introduced by Cal's ex-lover Tyffany Million—which shows you how close-knit the porn group is—and Cal told Jill he would be her guide into the business. Yet, after they were married, Cal suggested that they should get out of the industry. Jill agreed, but Cal then changed his mind and told her that only he would leave the business. He did, although their marriage was strained because Cal had no income and Jill's wages from adult films and dancing were paying all their bills. Cal got jealous of Jill and grew violent and possessive. Jill moved out. Cal went back into porn but because of drugs and personal problems he had difficulty with his performance. Cal's paychecks shrunk; he was used to getting $800 per scene in the prime of his career, but now he was accepting work for much less. When Cal and Jill were hired, separately, to do a porn shoot in Tahoe, it was Cal who was cut from the cast at the last minute. Meanwhile, Jill's career was taking off; Cal's problems continued. On the night of January 25, 1995, Cal Jammer pulled his car up to Jill Kelly's house, stood in her driveway, put a gun to his temple, and pulled the trigger. He was 34 years old.

While Cal and Jill's situation had its uniquely trying components, relationships can and do thrive in the adult industry. In the end, it is always about the resolve and commitment you have in making your partnership work. Some of porn's happy couples include Russ & Betty Hampshire, who both run the massively successful VCA Pictures, and Tim and Alyssa Lake, who run the huge amateur porn distribution company Homegrown Video.

C. MYTHS & REALITIES

1. Life as a Porn Star

"A Certain Kind of Fame." Undeniably, porn stars act out the sex fantasies for this, our great, God-fearing nation. Like rock singers, porn stars go out in front of people and try to give all of themselves. Like movie stars, they get in front of a camera and expose parts of their insides as well as their outsides. Public recognition comes with the certain kind of fame X will bring you. I say "certain kind of fame" because it's decidedly different than being, say, Tom Hanks. Sure, people will recognize you—in the grocery store, on the street, in a theater, in a dentist's office, and especially the video store. Yes, you might get to do the round of daytime talk shows like Oprah, Ricki Lake or Jerry Springer. Quite possibly, you might go on Howard Stern and raffle yourself off to a horny fan. But unlike Tom Hanks, you act out sexual pleasure for a living. And you will meet people who know that when they see you. It can be good and bad.

Everyone reacts to the fame differently—some love it, some hate it. Even if you do a few movies, pocket the cash to pay your bills, and get out, your movie will be in the AVN catalogue forever. You cannot hide anymore. You will go to Safeway and someone will recognize you, they will be looking at you and you will know they're looking at you because they've seen you get laid. Says director Gary Sage: "Some girls are unnerved by this. They can't handle it and it plays with their heads. Thus, the pressure and why some of them have to do drugs to cope with it."

On the other hand, porn girls Janine, Juli Ashton, Jenna Jameson, and Jill Kelly seem part of the New Porn Generation—strong, business-savvy porn starlets who more reflect the glamour of international models than the stereotype of skanky, strung-out and exploited head cases. They bask in their roles as porn's sexual ambassadors to the mainstream, which is as much a product of the aggressive marketing powers of the bigger studios that back them than anything else.

Performance Anxiety. Yes, there is this kind of pressure in being an adult film star. For the women, it's the fame, the money, or screwed-up motives for getting into the business in the first place. With men, it's a little more simple. Even the big, legendary Leading Lords of porn whose whole act revolved around a sort of 1970s laid-back, polyester smoothness—Harry Reems, John Holmes, Paul Thomas—were that way because they were good actors off as well as on-screen. In reality, they felt the performance anxiety as much as any budding soap or sitcom star. It was rumored that John Holmes didn't much enjoy sex to begin with—oral or otherwise. But like the women, there are a few great male examples of the New Porn Generation—Sean Michaels, Steven St. Croix, Bobby Vitale, Jeff Stryker, and Jon Dough among others—who seem to be tailor-made for this kind of fame. They grew up on MTV and the 80s revolution in video porn, and as a result, they seem more adaptable and amenable to the life of a porn star as a career option, along with being a carpenter or a BMW salesman.

Professionalism. I wrote in my earlier book, *The Big Bad Book of Sex Opportunities,* "Those of you who think you may be interested in the adult industry have to realize several important points. First, professionalism is just as important here as anywhere else. That means you groom yourself nicely, you behave courteously, and you show up where you're supposed to be on time." This has never been more true than now, when the World of X is attempting to put on its best Sunday clothes for mainstream America. But besides the PR angle, to not be a professional in this business is to be hated by the people who are striving to advance and upgrade the industry's image. Savannah was a prime example of a porn starlet who crossed the diva line way too many times: a $200-a-day junkie, she was frequently too strung out to dance her shows in strip clubs and often showed up late for her movie and photo shoots. When she did, she demanded everything from coffee to script approval. She got away with it because she was girl-next-store beautiful and her films sold up to 20,000 units each—five times that of regular porn films. Women like her are rare in porn, which is why they are so in demand, which is why they can get away with as much shit as they do. However, porn fame is not like Hollywood fame. Savannah's behavior didn't stop certain people in the Industry from calling her an "ice queen," a "cold bitch" or an "evil cunt." (And it didn't help her career that much, either.) When she died, Al Goldstein's *Screw* magazine, a sort of consumer rag for the East Coast adult scene, ran the headline "DING DONG, THE BITCH IS DEAD!"

As Savannah's example shows, and as we will discuss in the following section, different rules apply to both sexes. This is what two tried and true veterans of the business said to me about professionalism for male and female actors, respectively:

RANDY WEST: *Number one, you really have to be glad that someone's giving you a chance to do it. Don't come in cocky like you're Mr. Stud because most Mr. Studs are Mr. Duds. Just be glad you're getting some, and make sure it's something you really want to do because once you start doing it full time it really becomes like a sport. It's like being an athlete: you use your body a lot and it wears it out. You have to know how to pace yourself and space things out and come in with a professional mind—not just, "I'm getting' laid," but you have to understand how the whole thing is put together. It's business. If it wasn't, we'd all be out fucking in the street. But it's a business and you have to know how to take care of it and treat it like such. Show up on time, be clean, know how to take care of your own business, know how to treat people... If you do that you have a shot. It doesn't matter how big your dick is, it's whether you can get it up on cue or not.*

ASHLYN GERE: *You have to remember that if you're inside the business it's exactly that, a business, and we have no time for drugs or funny business. You're coming to work; be ready to work. As long as you give 110% and not lay there like a dead fish, if you are unique and don't look exactly like someone else already in the business, you have a very good chance of staying in and lasting for a long time. You have to want to be in this business for the right reasons, not the wrong ones. Like the money. Because then it plays with people's heads and they're out of the biz after six months.*

On the porn set or on the tube, Ashlyn Gere gives 110%.

Exploitation. The most misunderstood parts of today's adult industry are connected with the social stigmas that still plague it. "The biggest myth about the people in this business," says top porn agent Jim South, "is that we're all a bunch of pimps, hookers and drug addicts." One of the more stinging criticisms leveled at porn people is that they—meaning the women—are forced into sex work and are unaware that they are being exploited.

Much of this has to do with the early age of porn in the 70s, when laws regarding what was considered obscene were a little less well-defined than they are now. Porn makers all over the world frequently made films that depicted—however simulated—incest, violent rape fantasies, including S&M and bondage, and, in some cases, bestiality (sex with animals). Nowadays the depiction of any violent, non-consensual sex (i.e., bondage with hardcore sex), urination or defecation, and child pornography is illegal and the laws are strictly enforced—meaning, if you deal in this stuff, you will go to jail. There are 8,000 full-time cops in Los Angeles who monitor this arena, and because Los Angeles produces around 90% of America's porn, they are very good at what they do.

A lot of porn's stigma has more to do with its international reputation than anything occurring in the modern American sex industry. For a brief period—about four years—child pornography existed in various forms in underground publications in Denmark and Sweden. Some managed to be pirated to the United States. Then, partly in thanks to national revulsion in the U.S. at a 1984 NBC news special on child porn called *The Secret Shame*, stringent laws came crashing down and the international child porn racket was virtually extinguished. In fact, much of the child porn in America today is produced by the U.S. government in an effort to snag pedophiles who venture onto the Internet to locate kiddie-related enjoyables. For example, the Feds kept publishing *Wonderland*, a sort of networking magazine for pedophiles, long after the guy who published it had died!

Linda Lovelace, actually, is the link between a lot of porn myths. The star of the first mainstream porn film *Deep Throat*, she not only renounced her porn past but published several autobiographies saying how she was coerced—no, wait, forced—to perform her sexual acts onscreen. The most notorious was a destructive film for porn's reputation: *Dogarama*, (a.k.a. *Dog Fuck, Linda Lovelace and a Dog,* or *Dog I* and *Dog II*). Still available in peep shows in the Netherlands, this was a 16-minute home movie where she did exactly what you think she did on camera. Understandably, she tried to later distance herself from such things, saying in her 1980 book *Ordeal* that she was offered the choice—at gunpoint—of doing the pooch or dying. Her story was contradicted by a number of people. "She enjoyed that dog," Bill Margold, who saw the film, told me. "It was the dog that looked guilty." Still, Lovelace's published allegations that she was in sexual slavery on film helped to create the enduring myth that many women are forced against their will to appear in sex acts on (and off) the screen. She was, after all, the first American porn queen. A journalist even gave a name to the porn stars who radically renounce their past in order to gain acceptance from the mainstream entertainment world, calling it "The Linda Syndrome."

Porn's exploitative nature definitely exists—there are a lot of scumbags in the Industry that you should steer clear of (see section on 'How Not To Get Scammed'). Yet this advice is what anyone would give you even if you were going for a job in "regular" films: Beware of the casting couch! Before he became porn's biggest and most well-known agent, Jim South booked models for department-store ads and mail-order catalogues, and he claims to have witnessed more exploitation doing that than what he's seen in 25 years in the porn business.

Many other porn stars—male and female—echo this sentiment. In X, the casting couch is in front of the camera. If you have already gotten to the point where you feel comfortable having sex on camera for money, then you are that much more emotionally prepared. The odd thing about the porn world is that, if there is a casting couch, it is not forced on you. In fact, as you will see at the end of this chapter when a young friend of mine named Mariah encounters her first "auditions," people are quite up front and casual if they do want you to demonstrate your technique on them rather than on film. The important thing is that, as Nina Hartley emphasized to me, you do not need to be a victim to succeed in the World of X:

NINA HARTLEY: *Now, actually, at a certain level, it couldn't be a better time to get into the business as a young performer because the support system is in place. We have the Adult Industry Medical Health Care Foundation (AIM) and other things— there is support for young talent now that wasn't there before; there are veterans like myself who stay around and talk to new people and give them advice. There's absolutely no reason why you have to get fucked over or make the same mistakes we made in this business. We're here to go, 'No no no, THIS is how you handle it,' and they can build on our success and go further than we did, so to speak.*

The fact that I'm here and making it probably makes it more legitimate, meaning it attracts a higher caliber of people. So smart people are coming into the business, people who have had other careers elsewhere are coming into the business now and realizing, 'I want to be here!' Go see AIM and get info there, go get the tape Sharon and I made for new people in the Biz. Talk talk talk, read read read, there's lots of info out there, lots of books out there about it. There's no excuse for getting fucked over nowadays. There's plenty of information. Do your research. If a person is so clueless as to just jump in without thinking, they are probably not mature enough to handle it, to be in this business, to do this as a job.

2. A Day in the Life

Porn has been so endlessly compared to the glamour of Hollywood that many forget it requires effort to produce it. Sure, it's having sex and getting paid for it, but it's also a job. You still have to make the sex look like fun, even when you're not into it. Therein lies the challenge, the essential role of "acting," of being an adult performer. And your fans, believe it or not, can tell. Porn consumers want to see you have a genuinely good time—the whole point of them renting or buying your image is to benefit sexually from *your* experiences!

Apart from the reasons we've already discussed, the World of X is also different from most careers because it never sleeps. There are multiple movies being filmed every day in different parts of Los Angeles, and that's pretty much 24/7. Porn is being made on Christmas, New Years' Eve AND Day, and Yom Kippur; the only exceptions are the few "porno holidays" like the Consumer Electronics (CES) shows in Vegas and the Adult Video News (AVN) awards. Vivid girl Janine is probably the most popular porn star of the decade and even she works ten hour days. Jill Kelly is one of the more extreme examples of how much energy—and how strong a personality—is required to compete as a top adult performer. Jill described her work day to me as follows:

JILL KELLY: *Call time is 8am, so you drive in L.A. traffic to wherever the shoot may be—hopefully it's close by where you live. You get up at 5am, you take your shower, you shave your legs, you blow dry your hair, and you pack all your clothes. So you're out the door by 6:30. You get to the set at 8am, you're in the makeup chair until probably 9:30 or ten o'clock. Then you're on set and you're doing dialogue. Depending on how good an actress you are—if you're lucky, or unlucky like me, you're good with dialogue and you're appearing with someone who doesn't learn dialogue very well—you get saddled with the majority of the dialogue. So you shoot all the dialogue scenes and that maybe takes 2 to 2½ hours. Then you break for lunch for about an hour and then they're ready to film your sex scenes. Maybe you're doing an anal that day so you have to do an enema. Maybe it's taking a little bit longer than normal and everybody's finished their lunch and are waiting on you. You do your girl thing and then you go out and they start to shoot you. Then they have to do the softcore shots, then they have to do the hardcore shots, then they shoot the production stills—it takes on the average about an hour to shoot one sex scene. That's about 15-20 minutes of film. Every film is different too—Gonzo, a feature, whatever—and you're back and you have a costume change and then you're learning different dialogue and maybe the talent's an hour late, so maybe you're waiting on them. Then you shoot your other scenes and then you shoot your box covers. Then you're outta there at about 1am and you have another call at 8am the following morning, so you have to do it all over again.*

That's what my schedule used to be like. Now I go to the edit bay and oversee the films, take care of my business calls, start booking talent for my shoots that day or the next; the next day I might be going for an audition for a mainstream role, so then I have to rehearse for that audition. I have meetings all day Saturday. Usually Sundays

I fly out to New York, where I'm going to be dancing all week. I get in at 8pm and go to the hotel, I am three hours behind so I have to get used to the time change—and I have to do a show at noon the next day. And I have to get up earlier than that to get my makeup on and lay out my outfits from the trunks I bring along.

This year is actually the first year I've really taken more time off. I bought my house a year ago and I've probably been there a total of 30 days. But now that I have the live Internet camera at my ranch, I'm planning on staying home a lot more.

Jill Kelly teases us with her trademark heart-shaped tattoo.

Whew! Thanks, Jill! (We'll be hearing more from her again later in this book.) As you can see, the nuts-and-bolts side of being a sex worker is very much like carrying your lunch pail to the office five days a week. And it's fraught with the little annoyances that plague everyday people in everyday life albeit with an X-twist: your call time is 5 pm and they don't even start the scene until after midnight; you may have a perfectionist director who conducts long, grueling shooting sessions; the director gets into a fight with the cameraman; you are about to reach orgasm and some crew member's pager goes off and ruins the scene… you get the picture. The trick of porn is that the people watching the average sex scene can never know any of the hassles and nightmares of filming a sex scene. This is why it's called "acting."

Except, you'll notice, in porn there are no incidents of someone showing up to the workplace with an Uzi. Porn has had its share of tragedies, but no one ever complained that there was a lack of camaraderie on a porn shoot. "If you take all the people in the Industry, we're about the size of the U.S. Post Office," actor/director Randy West told *Los Angeles* magazine. "Compared to them, we do pretty well in the suicide department—and they usually take a lot of people with them."

The Porn Shoot. To be sure, the commercial production of pornography is about as un-erotic and manufactured as a professional wrestling match. Often, the biggest difficulties for the talent are the physical and emotional demands made on them. You have to watch a 15 to 20 minute sex scene and realize that it is not sex. Chances are that scene took anywhere from one to four hours to shoot, with periodic stops in the sex to adjust lighting, camera angle, and change sexual positions. And before that scene is shot, usually there are other photographers on set to take stills for various trade magazines like *Hustler Erotic Video Guide* (HEVG) or *Adam Film World* (AFW). Pictures are taken for the box cover of the film, too. They usually shoot the 'dialogue' scenes after that. Meanwhile, the art director may prepare the scene with some furniture, props, toys, and pillows. Many times, two kinds of films are shot at once, hardcore and softcore. Hardcore is the, pardon the expression, "balls out" version where everything is shown. The softcore version is the one where the film gets recut with no shots of penetration, erect penises, or semen. It typically is sold to cable and hotel pay-per-view channels.

There are a requisite number of positions that can be scheduled by the director, depending on what the talent has previously agreed to do or not to do. These include fellatio, cunnilingus, missionary-style, doggie-style, cowgirl (girl on top, man on back), reverse cowgirl (man on bottom, girl on top facing away), anal (doggie-style), double penetration (one penis in the vagina; one in the anus), double pussy penetration (two penises in the vagina), double anal penetration (two penises in the anus—yow!), anal cowgirl and, last but certainly not the least, reverse-anal cowgirl (woman on top facing away from the man, who is penetrating her anally). There are six basic sexual-partner combinations: solo masturbation, girl-girl, boy-girl, girl-girl-boy, boy-boy-girl, boy-boy, and (my personal favorite) the orgy. The really talented also can engage in fisting, like Filipina star Cumisha Amado or the notorious Viper. Then there's auto-fellatio—a man sucking on his own dick.

A porn shoot can last anywhere from one day to five days, depending on the budget and whoever is paying for it. Porn sets almost always run behind schedule. Talent could be on a set from 9 am to 2 am, with a 7 am call-back the next day. The director is usually no more than fifteen away from the performers' genitals at any time. Crew presence on a shoot can range from one cameraman to 20 or 30 people. High-end porn locations might be classy studios like Track Tech—which has multiple sets, air-conditioned sound studios, a prop warehouse and a plush lounge area for the talent, including lit-mirrors, showers, a full kitchen, color TV and VCR, couches and a snack bar. The Iverson Ranch, where many old Hollywood Westerns starring the likes of John Wayne, Gary Cooper and (gulp) Ronald Reagan were shot, is a more rustic location, but equally popular among the bigger budget productions. There are also porn studios in New York and San Francisco. Then again, there are the "one-day wonders"—hardcore shot in one day in someone's apartment (or even an unheated warehouse) for a modest budget. In these productions, the "studio" might simply be an empty room with a blanket strewn across the floor. One porn film, *Star Angel*, was filmed in a New Jersey house across the street from where Richard Nixon was living at the time!

The typical porn crew—camera operators, assistant directors, box-cover photographers and other "crew hogs"—does not have as good a time as you might think. Most of them have film school degrees and work on porn shoots between jobs in regular Hollywood studios. Porn shoots often give them immediate training in the techniques of filmmaking while a place like Sony Pictures would start them off making copies and getting coffee. Crew members quickly become blase about the sex that's occurring fifteen feet away. It's less "Wow! I get paid to watch cute chicks run around with no clothes on and get fucked!" than "Oh, great, I have to set up all the equipment and props and then sit around while some spoiled starlet holds up shooting by being a total raving bitch."

Crews are always working, even when the performers are sitting in their chairs taking their breaks. A crew on some of the larger sets can include: a director (who sometimes is also the cameraman), one or two camera operators, an art director, a boom operator, who dangles the long microphone over the set to catch the dialogue and moaning, a lighting technician, and a video deck operator (also known as the "deck tech"). All of them have to be quiet when the performers are going through their routines. Often there is also the producer running around the set in a panic. After all, it's his money being invested and it could be his ass thrown in jail if he doesn't have a shooting permit, copies of all of the performer's HIV tests, I.D.s, and signatures on their model release forms. The main thing is to remember that the people on the set are professionals who are counting on you to be likewise. "Everybody's there doing a job," Peter North explained to me. "No one's there judging you. They want you to be as good as you want to be. The only pressure on you is the kind you put on yourself. They'll try to make everything as comfortable as possible for you and you just have to get into the moment. Block everything out and concentrate on the person you're going to be working with. It's a lot of mind over matter."

Of course, there are limits on how far the crew will go to accommodate your needs. "Fluffers," or young women who offer fellatio to the male talent to prepare them for a sex scene, are mainly a thing of the past. John T. Bone's *World's Biggest Gang Bang* series featured fluffers on their gang bang sets. (The Houston 500 gang bang actually produced a spin-off video entitled *The Fluff Girls of the Houston 500*—so maybe "fluffing" is coming back.) In a lot of older porn films from the 70s, sometimes the man will have an erection at the beginning of a scene rather than his leading lady bringing him to arousal on camera. But most modern porn directors are on too tight of a budget to afford fluffers.

D. PORN PROFILES: ENTERING THE PLAYPEN
(Interviews with Bill Margold, Henri Pachard, Jim South, Mariah Wind, and Max Hardcore)

1. Bill Margold and P.A.W.

If it seems like you've read the name "Bill Margold" a few hundred times so far, that's because there's rarely any discussion about pornography where Margold's name *doesn't* surface. Since 1971, he's been a prominent fixture in the porn business, working as a performer, writer, producer, director, journalist, critic, and agent. He has had sex exactly 500 times on camera and claims to have only failed to get an erection twice—once in 1973 and once in 1986.

After the suicides of Savannah and Alex Jordan, Bill decided to start Protecting Adult Welfare (P.A.W.), a counseling service for troubled porn performers that has gotten a lot of praise for providing a much-needed service. Of course, Bill gets criticized by many people. He's been called an "asshole" and a "joke," and P.A.W. has been derided as just another way horny males can get in touch with the hot babes of the X-industry. (Bill has admitted as much.) But what matters is that P.A.W. is there for you if you need it—and Bill Margold is there to listen and give you all of the tough-love advice he has collected over his nearly 30 years in the porn world. He talks to anybody about the X-rated business because he has nothing to hide. The thing about Bill you should know before you meet

Just like his "kids," Bill Margold loves all his bears equally.

him is that he will give you more reasons why you shouldn't be entering the Business of X rather than why you should. He practices hard, tough love—not the physical but the emotional kind. He figures about 90% of the kids who come to see him do not go onto a career in X.

There is nothing sexual about Bill's office at P.A.W. The only thing remotely reminding anyone of the X-rated industry is a poster Bill did for the Free Speech Coalition—a group of well-oiled babes, including his ex-lover Viper, hoisting the American flag a la Iwo Jima. (He calls it "my greatest creation.") He keeps an army of teddy bears in his office to be hugged by those who need them. Bill doesn't have favorite bears ("That would be unfair to the other bears"), but there is a bear in his apartment who has become the mascot of the X-rated industry: Mr. Bearson Stubbs. "If the kids fall out of the tree of X," Bill says, "they know I am always here to catch them." It was Bill who, in 1985, took in a destitute Harry Reems. Once the highest-paid actor in porn, Reems had spent the first part of the 80s bouncing in and out of mental institutions, detox centers and jail cells. Reems credited Bill for saving his life.

If you decide to visit Bill, he will put you through a laundry ringer of questions that is like a verbal boot camp of what one is to expect from, as Bill refers to it, the "Circus of X." He will fire questions at you like tennis balls: What's your educational background? What are your plans? Do you have any aspirations? What are your parents going to think? Do you feel you owe your parents anything? Are you going to hurt anyone by doing this? Do you have any children? Do you understand what will be expected of you in this business?

When Bill invited me to drop in on his office at P.A.W., I began by asking what advice he would give my readers.

BILL MARGOLD: Consider the world of X like the island of Madagascar in the game of Risk: the harder it is to get to there, the better off we are. I like it that way. The more tolerant we become, the more allowed we are, the more absorbed into the mainstream we become, the quicker chance we have of going down the drain and I don't like that. I want to remain the enigma, the mystique, the outlaw. The outlaw is a very important statement, even today. That's what makes X the most magnificent letter in the entertainment alphabet.

ANA LORIA: *You come from a Probation officer background where you watched over the troubled inner city kids of Los Angeles. How did you get into the adult film industry?*

BILL: I immediately sensed that this is where I belonged because these people reminded me of the kids I worked with in juvenile hall. They were all in this sort of perpetual, against-the-grain state of rebellion. And I fell in love with them and adopted them. I became their daddy, or uncle, or brother.

ANA: *Why do you try to discourage people from getting into porn?*

BILL: What is up against the kids getting into the business now is even greater than before, because this industry has become more and more like a meat grinder, where these poor children get dumped head-first and are ground up and come out as by-products. This is why I don't think people who are 18-20 are ready to come into this business [because they] have no clue how to protect themselves. In a sense they don't even want to be protected. They all walk in here thinking they're gonna be stars and the real world's going to accept them with open arms and legs; they'll use us as a springboard into mainstream Hollywood. What exactly are [superstarlets] like Jenna Jameson? They are this year's two-headed dog. This year's pet rock. This year's hula hoop. The real world will simply use your image for its purposes and throw you away. The primary image of all that is Ron Jeremy. The man most used by the real world and the most untolerated man by that world at the same time. Do you *really* want to be Ron Jeremy when you grow up?

I've gone through a series of roommates—'children' as I call them, since the majority of my kids are overage juvenile delinquents. I do not have sex with the people I put up here, since I'm not into incest. But I love them, and I will watch over them and protect them until they feel they no longer need it. The parent tree of X, which begins with me, has spawned an awful lot of cubs who set up their own trees—but all of those cubs can come home to the parent tree if they want it. Nina Hartley's a cub. Sharon Mitchell's a cub. Even my worst cubs—the ones who are rotten to the core, the ones who I have helped and who have turned on me—know they can come back to the tree. I cannot deny any of them; I'm not allowed to. These people are way down deep, very innocent, and they want to be children again.

I think it is unfair to bring this business into the real world and expect the real-world person to put up with it—unless the real-world person is what we call a 'suitcase pimp.' A lot of girls will allow themselves to be in relationships where the man is the dominant, dictatorial, almost brutalizing force in their lives. The girls are guaranteed to go home and be mistreated—essentially punished for what they're doing.

There's a lot of self-destruction in the industry—just as there is in the music industry or the mainstream-movie industry. Because no matter how successful you are in the X-rated industry there's always going to be a moment when you fail. There's going to be a part you don't get, there's going to be a scene when you can't get it up. There's going be someone who is chosen over you for a role. There's going to be someone who comes along who is going to damn you for what you've done. Even the most ethereal, benign, magnificent bowl of sunshine like Nina Hartley, I'm sure, at one time or another has been scorned or suffered the slings and arrows of an accusatory, derogatory slam.

ANA: *What is the end result of having a career in this business?*

BILL: Believe it or not, doing something for society in general. You're serving a purpose—you are getting society off.

ANA: *Do people really have a tangible end goal in mind?*

BILL: No, because I don't think they're going to stay in it for any great length of time. I think this is a passing fancy in most people's minds. Power is transient in this business.

2. A Day at World Modeling Agency

The same day I visited Bill, he took me to World Modeling Agency to meet Mariah Wind, a 21-year-old Latina single mother with a gorgeous body who wanted to get into the adult industry. She had already survived two meetings with Bill unscathed and undaunted to pursue her goal of fame and glory as a porn actress. Since she had to drive into L.A. from suburban Ontario, she arrived a little late, and I ended up first chatting with one of the legendary directors of porn, Henri Pachard. Mr.

Pachard, who often comes by the offices of World Modeling to check out the new talent, is one of the few members of the porn industry who has spoken up publicly about raising the minimum age of a performers to 21, which just happens to be how young Mariah Wind is. (Note: For a detailed explanation of World Modeling, please see Chapter Two.)

ANA: *Can you tell me as a director what you look for in talent?*

HENRI PACHARD: I like my talent to be able to bring something to the table, rather than just ask me what I want them to do and how do I want them to do it. If they are given a role to play, they own the character. I want them to come back and bring me something that I can work with and get the other characters to react to, rather than just come in with their pockets empty. I want them to be willing to take risks.

ANA: *Can you give me an example? Like the top five male actors of all time sort of thing?*

HENRI: Joey Silvera was always a tremendous explorer of characters, and John Leslie, of course, who in his prime as an actor was undoubtedly the most extraordinary actor I ever worked with. There was also Jerry Butler—unpredictably gifted. Paul Thomas and Randy Spears... those five could take characters and make something happen; they were all actors. They were fun to work with. You never knew what they were going to do. I didn't have to worry about them and I could then concentrate on somebody else who might be struggling with it.

I mean, we all know what we're going to see in an adult movie or video, right? Everybody knows what they are going to see, but they have no idea what they are going to hear. So I can remove the predictability of the scene by their behavior during the actual sex scene. I gave them a specific character, a direction to go, goals to have, words to say. I like to be surprised by my talent. I don't need to hear how 'good' it feels; if anything, say 'ouch.' And don't just lay there getting a blow job—fuck the woman's mouth. Don't bore me with romance! Fill me up with a sense of shame, make me feel I shouldn't be watching this. Things like that.

Observing the actresses can be really interesting, too. They would come from a background of hooking or stripping, or both, and when they got into adult films they'd be very concerned when they were told they had to learn dialogue and be a character and all that. Inevitably, 90% of them really fell into it. They discovered the joys of role-playing just like they did when they were children. They'd forgotten all of that. It's wonderful to see some confused girl from the street all of a sudden discover a sense of dignity she'd never experienced before.

[Mariah Wind finally arrives and apologizes for being late. She looks like a tinier

version of actress/singer Jennifer Lopez and she is dressed to kill in a black lace body-suit under a short black skirt. Jim South, who runs World Modeling Agency, explains to her a few things to watch out for in the porn business, especially that breed of reptile called the "suitcase pimp."]

JIM SOUTH: These are guys who usually start out as talent and they can't do good, and they end up getting, for example, your phone number, Mariah. They take you out to dinner or have coffee with you and they promise you the world and tell you whatever agency they're with, it doesn't matter who it is, they aren't doing the right job for you. 'Gosh, you only got $900 on your last boy-girl?! I can get you a lot more than that' which they usually do. Then they encompass the girl very much like a pimp would; they set up the work, they negotiate the money, they find out what they're supposed to take, they find out where they're supposed to go, then they tell her they have her work. But for this, they usually charge 20% of what they make, which they collect directly from the girl, where the girl can get the same job through an agency and not pay anything.

BILL MARGOLD: Porsche Lynn actually came up with the term suitcase pimp, because a lot of these guys will walk behind the girl carrying her bags. They are essentially leeches. It's a reverse form of Japanese subservience.

ANA: *What kind of questions did they ask you when you first came down to World Modeling, Mariah?*

MARIAH WIND: They just asked me my name and my age and whether I had ever done this before.

ANA: *Had you?*

MARIAH: Nope, never. Not even one scene yet. I've been dancing around the country for five years. I also have my own phone sex line.

JIM: Well, after a while, after a quick while, everybody will have your number, everybody will start calling you direct, and you won't have to deal with us so much again.

MARIAH: Okay.

JIM: And if you are reliable for one director, then he's going to go and tell two other directors and it just expands that way, by word-of-mouth.

ANA: *What made you want to get into this business, Mariah?*

Newcummer Mariah Wind struts her stuff on the beach.

MARIAH: Well, it all started when I went to an adult yard sale.

ANA: *A what?*

MARIAH: An adult yard sale. It's where they sell porno movies for cheap and stuff. I went there to do a little promoting for myself—you know, give out a few of my phone-sex cards and sell a few t-shirts. I had met Bill Margold, and just started talking to him about doing movies. Plus, I love money and I love attention, so I had made an appointment to see him and he took me to Jim South.

ANA: *What kind of questions did you have for Bill when you met with him?*

MARIAH: I didn't have any because I already know what I want.

ANA: *What's that?*

MARIAH: I want it all! *[Laughs]*

ANA: *Did you make any audition tapes?*

MARIAH: No.

ANA: *What did Bill tell you when you went to him?*

MARIAH: Just what was in store for me. I said, 'Okay.' He told me I shouldn't go in head first. I'm not just going to go right in and start doing movies. I'm taking little baby steps, like when I start out I'll just do blowjobs and some girl-girl movies. Maybe a little modeling, stuff like that.

ANA: *Are you going to start with the modeling first?*

MARIAH: Both films and modeling. I'm doing my first sex scene on Monday.

ANA: *Are you nervous?*

MARIAH: Yeah and no. But I like the attention, so I'm actually looking forward to it!

ANA: *Do you know who you're going to be working with beforehand?*

MARIAH: Yeah, they told me. I forgot his name. We actually don't know if he's going to be able to do it or not. But I'll know by then, when I get there I guess. I'm going to talk to them tomorrow.

ANA: *Is it one scene?*

MARIAH: Yeah, just boy-girl.

ANA: *Did they tell you to bring anything?*

MARIAH: Just whatever I'm going to wear, and that's it.

ANA: *How do you think dancing prepared you for this next step?*

MARIAH: Just being out there. Getting to know the men and what they want to hear and what they want me to do.

JIM: A lot of the directors are veterans, and a lot of these guys want you early, when you're just starting out. So we try to get you out there quickly, twice a week we e-mail your image with all the information you gave us to about 40 to 50 of my biggest clients. It's more valuable for you that they get you first.

MARIAH: Okay.

JIM: *[To me]* What's important to me about the people I provide talent for, first, is the way they treat the talent. Second, do they pay them what they're supposed to be paid? Third, do they pay the agent's fee? Other than that I don't have a problem with them at all. Anytime someone says, 'Jim's got a problem with me, he doesn't like me—that's why he never gets me work.' That's not true. It's always business.

[To Mariah] If I sent you to people who verbally or physically mistreated you or people who bounce checks, then I'm not doing my job. I'm not just saying this to you because you're new, but you have to care. If you don't—get out of this business. We don't need you.

MARIAH: Alright.

3. In the Offices of P.A.W.

Bill Margold's Protecting Adult Welfare is right down the hall from World Modeling and its suite of offices. Mariah, Bill and I are waiting around for the directors to come in and start Mariah's first round of job interviews.

BILL: This is the third time [Mariah and I] have met. After the first time, the yard sale, I called her bluff: my kids have to call me; I don't call them. When she did call me, I exactly remembered who she was and where we met, which surprised her. But I remember everyone that I meet. Particularly brand new ones. In those three times I tried to convince her not to do this. First off, she has a kid, a 2-year-old girl, nice little kid, and her mother apparently is tolerating what she is doing.

ANA: *Is your kid coming to you 20 years from now holding one of your videos or magazines something you see as a problem?*

MARIAH: No. She won't be complaining. She'll have all the things she needs—all the things I want her to have that I couldn't, you know? If my mom was doing that for me, I wouldn't complain.

BILL: Ah, that's funny, because if everything works out, in January or maybe even as early as November, we'll bring Mariah and mom to Las Vegas to go to a convention. And if the mother's any good we'll put her to work, too.

MARIAH: *[Laughs]* She's kinky, but…

BILL: Well, there are over-40 and over-50 magazines.

ANA: *How did you tell your mom about this, Mariah?*

MARIAH: Well, she's known for awhile. When I turned 18, I told her I wanted to dance nude, she told me then like she's told me all the time: 'Just don't forget about me.'

BILL: What does that mean exactly?

MARIAH: I think she means money-wise.

BILL: Oh, you see I don't like that. I would sooner call her bluff and put her in the business. Then she'd make her own money.

MARIAH: Well, she was telling me, 'Let me be your manager.'

BILL: What does she know about managing a career in this Industry?

MARIAH: Nothing.

BILL: Well, hopefully you're headstrong enough that you don't need anybody in that respect taking money from you.

MARIAH: Well, I wouldn't let her be no manager.

BILL: But if she wants to get into the business on her own—not sex but nude modeling or something like that—there are magazines that would just chew her up, just love her. They'll pay her good money for just doing nude layouts. If she has big tits—I expect she's an older version of you with big tits, right?

MARIAH: Well, she's kinda overweight.

BILL: They don't care.

MARIAH: She looks like me with glasses.

BILL: They don't care about any of that. As long as she can validate her age, the older-woman magazines would just eat her up…

MARIAH: When she found out how much I made at phone sex—about $1,000 every week and a half—she wanted to quit her job and do phone sex full time! When I was dancing I could take home like $900 on a good night. But I've gone home with $200 a night. Hell, I've gone home with $2 in one night! Because you have to pay out—you're actually paying them to do the dance there.

ANA: *How much do they usually charge?*

MARIAH: Depends on how many dances you get. They take ten dollars out of each dance. For couch dances that are totally nude, which run about $40, they would take $15. And you have to pay the waitress and the doorman, too.

BILL: Yeah, but there's a lot more money out there than just those things. You are a little too good for just phone sex, my dear.

MARIAH: Well, you've gotta do a lot of your own promotion. You have to go out there and make yourself known. *[to Bill]* Like when I met you passing out the cards.

BILL: Yep. You were out there working it, and that's what I immediately liked about you. Your energy. 'I will not be denied.' But you also have a logical reason for why you're doing this: for the fame and attention. *[Mariah prepares to change into some lingerie.]* It's okay child, you can change in front of us. Don't be embarrassed to be 'bare-assed.' Are you scared of showing your breasts?

ANA: *I can close the door.*

BILL: Yes, go ahead—so we don't put on a show. But I liked her because she was against the grain: she's short, her breasts are in excellent shape, and I don't even like tits; and she has a desire to do this. I think that's what it takes. Whether she is 'born hot' I don't really know—but she's born adventurous and that does suggest a potential future for her in this business. I don't think the Industry will be able to take advantage of her as long—and I've told her this—she consults me on what she's doing and what she's being asked to do; she was worried because she went off and saw someone without asking me. *[Mariah laughs.]* I'm not her agent, but I'm trying to save her from the maximum amount of involvement in this business while still getting the maximum amount of money for her. Because she's starting off at $600 a scene—which she deserves—and probably $450 for girl-girl. This is not a bad-looking woman. The tattoo I don't care for, especially since she's thinking of having something added to it that will make it go all the way around her arm.

MARIAH: Yeah, I was thinking a band all the way around my arm. So wouldn't I be known as 'Mariah with a band'? *[Laughs]*

BILL: No, I think one band around your other arm with the name 'Mariah Wind' on it, maybe in silver or black. That's just my opinion. I think she's going to be fun. If she's not immersed in the business, drowned or overwhelmed by it. I will try to protect her from that. What you're doing for her is very beneficial because you are paying attention to her on a non-sexual level. You are allowing her to express her opinions on why she wants to do this and she's about as new as you're going to get. She's already being doing phone sex so that gives her a certain sexuality that puts her ahead of a lot of the other women. At least she knows how to "play the game" at a certain creative level.

MARIAH: Yep. I know what men want to hear.

BILL: Yep, talking about it can definitely expand your mind.

MARIAH: I mean, not what *every* one wants to hear, but I've gotten a taste. I've gotten a couple weird calls.

ANA: *Like what?*

MARIAH: This one guy called and had a fetish for enemas. 'Did you do you daily thing today?' 'Yeah, baby, I did it.' *[Laughs]* I had a guy who literally calls from a pay phone. I asked him what he was wearing and he said, 'Just my trench coat and my diaper.' We got a guy who's a teacher who calls when the kids are out on the playground during lunch. I got a guy who I sat on the phone with for three hours and I could not get him off. So, I'm talking with him for awhile and he says, 'Well, I know you're not there alone.' So now I had to pretend that my boyfriend's there. Eventually, what made him come was my boyfriend's dick in his mouth. I said, 'Well if I had known that's what you liked I would have done that from the beginning.' *[Laughs]*

BILL: Yeah, so she knows what men want to hear. *[To Mariah]* It would be good to talk a lot when you are doing your sex scenes with these guys, because that's about the only thing that's going to keep their interest while the sex is going on. Or ease them through—like a blind pig, until they find that proper sexual truffle. It could work out very, very nicely. Mariah is pretty, and she is pretty secure. What's interesting is that for her size she presents a bigger image than 5'3"—I like that, there's a lot of sexual presence there and it's very amusing. The original name I was going to give Mariah was 'Taffy,' and that's not to be denigrating her or anything. She has a nice, soft, comfortable-looking body. And like I say I don't like breasts, but hers look good. They are all natural but they have an almost bought-out-of-a-store look. Now I warned her that, thanks to gravity, they won't stay that way. Unless she wears good bras. Purple and black are the colors she looks best in, so I told her to go out and buy a few purple and black lingerie sets and be seen in that kind of outfit. Because her tits will go, you should also swim and exercise.

MARIAH: Yeah, I exercise a lot at home. I don't go to a gym or anything.

BILL: But you are not going to be a 'hardbody.'

MARIAH: No.

BILL: I don't think it's going to work. But there are things you can do to keep on top of your game. Very rarely do I tell people they need breast jobs and that's only if they've been damaged badly by having kids or they just need to be lifted because they sag too much.

ANA: *Who pays for that? The studio?*

BILL: No, you go get yourself a couple of jobs, pick up 3 or 4 grand and have 'em done. I'm not a fan of things being put into the body, I don't like things being corrected on the body.

ANA: *So Mariah is getting $600 for a "standard scene." What does that involve?*

BILL: It probably will start off with a blowjob, then hopefully he reciprocates and goes down on you—if you like oral sex and the guy knows what he's doing you probably will get off during that. Then the penetration scene will probably start off with 'spooning,' which is you facing the camera being fucked from behind. There is also 'cowgirl,' which you like, because you like getting on top of somebody and getting off that way. Or 'reverse cowgirl' where your face will be out towards the camera; 'doggy' style, which I think is the best of all positions because it's a really easy thing to shoot between all those legs.

MARIAH: No anal, though. Never.

BILL: Nope, no anal, no fisting. And with the money, to be honest with you the trick in this business is to consider it "found" money—meaning put half of it away, put half of everything you earn away. When you're done earning it, you have a lot of money put away that you can now then do something with. Don't spend every cent you make.

MARIAH: Okay.

BILL: It was very nice of this guy who paid for your HIV test—whether or not he deducts it from your $600, that's his prerogative. He can if he wants to. You had your blood taken yesterday over at AIM, right?

MARIAH: Yeah.

BILL: You can call over and see if the results are ready today.

MARIAH: Yeah, I think I'll do that.

ANA: *You said she should save half of everything she makes, but what about the expenses for her career. What kind of stuff does she need to buy, like new clothes, new makeup?*

BILL: Mariah's lucky. The less make-up she wears the prettier she is. She has that natural quality about her. And she's clean, too. She has very good teeth, which I am delighted by.

ANA: *What stuff should she buy?*

BILL: Well, if I were a bright performer I would go out and buy my own sex toys, toys I am comfortable with. If I had some favorite dildos or vibrators that I knew fit into me well I would use those, and I would spend the money on them to feel good—rather than take the chance of having a bunch of junk put into me that I may not know where it came from. Uh, tasteful lingerie. You should bring three changes of clothes to the set, even if you don't need it. Because they may shoot stills on her…I'd also bring my own lubricant, one that I like.

ANA: *Mariah, would you ever have a relationship with someone in the business?*

MARIAH: I don't think so.

BILL: That is something you cannot predict. You haven't met enough people to know that.

MARIAH: Well, in my mind—I see them having any girl they want, why would they want me?

BILL: Why wouldn't they?

MARIAH: I feel so different compared to most of the girls. Most of them all look alike; their bodies all look alike.

BILL: Yes, but that will make you more desirable in their eyes.

MARIAH: They look like they are made for this type of thing.

BILL: And so will you. Once you get a couple of these things under your belt you will eventually look much more confident than you do now when you realize that you can compete with these people. You will get that validation and you will start to glow.

ANA: *What about the adult press and things of that sort? When will they start doing stuff on her as a new talent?*

BILL: What will happen is that AVN will come to some set you are on, and then they'll interview you for one of their 'Fresh meat' sections or whatever; you'll tell them a little story about yourself. I can take care of that, but I want to get your first scene under your belt so you can tell us what you thought of this, then I'll send you to somebody.

MARIAH: So I go to the one on Monday and then tell you how it went?

BILL: Yes. You may not like it, but I suspect you will. Who are you going to be working with?

MARIAH: 'Howard.'

BILL: Is 'Howard' going to fuck you?

MARIAH: No, no, no, I don't think so.

ANA: *So who's the lucky guy?*

MARIAH: I picked him. I don't know his name, that's why I have to call them tomorrow.

ANA: *Did they give you a choice of which men to work with?*

MARIAH: No, no. He wants me to do a guy-girl, but he told me that most of his stuff is when the girl's sucking on his dick, so I don't know what's going to happen.

BILL: Yes, you do. You have to tell me what you found out.

MARIAH: But he let me see the guy's picture.

BILL: Did you like what the guy looked like?

MARIAH: He was alright. I'm not too fond of white boys.

BILL: You don't like white guys?

MARIAH: No, I do. But I like black and Latino guys better.

BILL: There are no Mexicans in this business. Maybe it has a moralistic bent to it. Being Catholic, maybe it's something they don't want to be involved with.

MARIAH: All the Mexicans I've been with, they never had a problem with me dancing.

BILL: How many guys have you been with?

MARIAH: About fifty, I think.

BILL: When did you start?

MARIAH: Fifteen. A lot of them were like in a year and a half because I was partying a lot and I had a lot of one-night stands. I've only had like five relationships.

BILL: Are you in one now? You said you had a couple of boyfriends.

MARIAH: Just dating.

BILL: And both of these boyfriends wish you well with your career?

MARIAH: Yeah, I wonder why they haven't called me. *[Laughs loudly]* Just kidding! My ex-boyfriend, I saw him today, and he's like, 'Where you goin'?' and I said, 'Oh, just to this job interview, and he goes, 'You're doin' the porn films, right?' He said it was cool with him, but you never really know. I don't know if he meant that. I have to talk to him again and see what he thinks about it because that's the guy I was engaged to. We were going to get married, but we broke up because I went back to dancing.

BILL: If he didn't like your dancing, he's not going to like your fucking.

MARIAH: But he didn't have a problem with the phone sex thing.

BILL: Well, nobody sees you and nobody touches you.

MARIAH: Well, I love him and I would like to spend the rest of my life with him, but I'm going to do this with or without him.

BILL: What about your birth control? Did you talk to the girls at AIM about this?

MARIAH: Yeah, I'm just waiting because I'm on my rag. I talked to her about the diaphragm. She gave me a bunch of different birth controls.

BILL: Don't take the pill. Use a diaphragm. It'll modulate your sexual involvement and it's not bad for your body. Sponges just chew up a guy's dick.

MARIAH: The sponges are where they put that foam in it that kills the sperm off?

BILL: Yeah. But again it eats up guy's dicks. And the guys aren't allowed to complain in this business. They are extremely lucky to be there.

MARIAH: This guy Howard was anxious when I met him. I walked in and he said, 'Oh, you're perfect! How about Monday—no, wait, Sunday?' *[Laughs]* I told him, 'Wait! I don't have my HIV test yet!'

4. Max

At around 3pm the World Modeling offices are abuzz—another legend is in the building: Max Hardcore. He looks like a short, mean Australian cowboy in his khaki shorts, hiking boots and ten-gallon cowboy hat. His hardcore anal films are often brutal, aggressive, and highly influential. With the exception of John Stagliano, no director has gotten more ripped off for all of the innovations he brought to porn than Max Hardcore. Which is why he was predictably leery when I asked to interview him in an empty side office at World Modeling.

ANA: *What will you ask Mariah when she comes in to interview with you?*

MAX: *[Coughs]* Whether she'll take it up the ass. Basically.

ANA: *Do you have a laundry list of things that you ask her if she'll do or not?*

MAX: No. I just tell them straight up—I mean, it's not the first thing I mention. I ask 'em if they like to fuck.

Porn cowboy Max Hardcore rides a pig-tailed Julianna Sterling.

ANA: *Isn't that kind of redundant? I mean, if they're already here?*

MAX: No, it's not redundant at all because most girls—correction: *all girls*—are whores; it's just a matter of price. So I have to figure out what the price is. 'Have you taken it up the ass before or not?' If they have, that could be a problem; if they haven't, that's good. That means you can show 'em how to do it, right? What is this thing you're writing for?

ANA: *Just a book on how to get into the adult industry. It's intended to be simple, objective, and non-judgmental.*

MAX: Uh-huh. Lemme explain something to you. We are in a business that most normal folks consider pretty unsavory, and most of the time, quite often, when people write about the Industry, it's in a negative light so we are justifiably leery of people coming in and writing about us because it's not gonna do any fuckin' good whatsoever to talk to you. It's not gonna help me sell any more videotapes. And it can cause problems. So we are a little reluctant to be totally open and explain the business, because what the fuck good is it gonna do me, Ana? If I tell you how I do the business?

I can tell you this much: one of the primary reasons to my success as a director is getting the girls to do things that prior to them working for me, they would never even consider doing with their boyfriends or husbands of 20 years, and they're gonna do that with me the first time we have sex. That's the difference between the great success that I enjoy and the marginal success most people who come through this business experience. It's a matter of fact. So it doesn't do me any good to tell people how I do it. Even if I did they wouldn't get it, because people try to copy me and my style of shooting and the aggressive behavior that I demonstrate on camera, and they still can't fucking get it. You can't just copy a master and hope that it's going to look as good. It doesn't. It looks stupid.

But it still affects my business because nowadays anybody who can figure out where the 'on/off' switch is on a video camera considers themselves a fuckin' director or a producer. And they don't have the first fuckin' idea what it takes to make the high-quality, intense pornography that we do.

ANA: *What do you want your potential talent to know before they come see you?*

MAX: Well, the ability to read and write helps, although it's not necessary. To have a car and know how to drive is a plus. Beyond that they don't need to know anything. The sad fact is that most girls don't know what they want until you tell them what they want. Then they get with the program.

ANA: *Is it almost better to come in cold like that and just be kind of open to new things?*

MAX: Well, you've got to want to do it. You've got to have the desire, no matter what. It's immensely helpful. Most of the girls in this business have pretty high sex drives—they like to fuck. However, if they're doing it just for the money that can be okay too, if they're good actresses. That accounts for about 50% of the girls in the business; the other 50% really like to fuck. A miscellaneous few don't know what the fuck they want. I've seen it all, and I tell you it never fails to fuckin' amaze me.

ANA: *Are there any myths you'd like to dispel for those wanting to get into the business?*

MAX: Well, I'm not in the myth-dispelling business, but I know that I had no clue. I came out here for the first time ten years ago. To tell you the truth, I thought there was more money in it than there is. Second, I thought it was a little better organized than it is. Of course, things have changed in ten years. There are a lot more people, a lot more shooters, because again with the advent of inexpensive camcorders and that whole 'Gonzo/Amateur' thing, everybody's getting in on the program. It's no help to me because it's just more competition and it's screwed up the prices with the girls. They're getting astronomical fees for doing this. When I started out 10 years ago, believe it or not, I was paying these whores $250 bucks for an all-day affair. Now these whores are making $1,000 an hour, and that is plain ridiculous. It's a simple matter of supply-and-demand. There's not enough good-looking whores to go around and there's too many shooters. I wish they'd go away and stay away and not bother me.

ANA: *What's your ideal female talent?*

MAX: Small, thin, bubbly personality, little bit nutsy, and fucks like the Eveready Bunny.

ANA: *How about male talent?*

MAX: Ideal male performer is someone who keeps his mouth shut and his dick hard. *[Leans forward to speak directly into tape recorder.]* Period.

5. Mariah After Her First Porn Shoot
The following Tuesday, I phoned Mariah Wind at her home to find out how her first-ever sex scene turned out.

MARIAH: Actually, Bill told me to tell you what happened. I had a little "experience" when I was being interviewed.

ANA: *What do you mean?*

MARIAH: Well, Bill was meaning to tell me that I probably was going to be offered a little bit more than doing movies. Like doing the directors.

ANA: *He didn't prepare you for that?*

MARIAH: No, he didn't mention that. But I guess he knew something like that was eventually going to come up, but he just thought, 'Oh, she has a good head on her shoulders; maybe she'll know right from wrong,'—which I do. I'm a very smart girl.

ANA: *Of course!*

MARIAH: I got interviewed by two [directors]. The first guy, a black guy, asked me to take a hardcore picture and I was like, 'What do you mean?' and he said, 'I want to take a picture of you giving me a blowjob.' So I told him, 'You're crazy! I don't do that, I'm sorry.' And he just said, 'Okay.' And I just walked out. The second guy, the one with the cowboy hat, took me into his office and was being really, like pervertish. Like he was rubbing on himself while he was talking to me—I thought *that* was really rude! But he was asking me if I did anal, and I said no. I'm not a girl for anal; I've never even done it with any of my boyfriends. He said, "Well that's what most of the girls say; we could practice." I said "What do you mean 'practice'?" and he said, "Well, we could practice right here; lemme stick it in your asshole." I looked at him like he was nuts. He's like, 'What, what do you mean?' He started getting mad so I changed the subject. I showed him some of my pictures, and then he kept on staring at me. He finally said, "You wanna fuck?" I just looked at him: "I'm sorry, but who do you think I am? I have a good head on my shoulders, I'm a very smart girl, I'm doing this because I like attention and I like money and I admit that, but that doesn't mean I'm a prostitute." So he's like, "I'll give you $40 to give me a blowjob." So I got up to leave and he said, "Well I'll never use you in any of my movies"; and I turned around and looked at him and said, "So, you are one out of how many?"

Jim South was getting worried. We were in that room for so long because he was trying to get me to have sex with him. That's why it took so long. But Jim had thought I had already done something with him. I walked into Bill's office and shut the door and said, "You never told me I was in store for this." Bill smiled at me and said, "Well, I didn't think I would have to tell you. I knew you were a very smart girl and you would know right from wrong." I said, "I do and I'm very proud of myself" and he's like "I'm proud of you, too!" and I go, "Well, you better walk in there and tell Jim South that if he thinks I did something in there with him, that he's wrong." So Bill did exactly that, and everybody in the office was all proud of me. They even clapped!

ANA: *Did that experience kind of freak you out?*

MARIAH: No, it made me stronger in my mind. It actually made me know what I'm in store for. If there are any producers out there who think I'm going to sleep with them just to get in their video, they're wrong. Like today I had interviews with a few producers and people like that and I told them, "I don't do agents, producers, directors or even cameramen!"

ANA: *Were you pissed off at Bill for not telling you that?*

MARIAH: No! He doesn't need to tell me. I know I have a really good sense of intuition, I guess. If I know something's wrong, I'm going to say it. I speak my mind.

ANA: *Were you nervous the night before your first scene?*

MARIAH: No, and I wasn't really nervous actually doing the scene either.

ANA: *They called you on Saturday and told you what time to show up and all that?*

MARIAH: Yep.

ANA: *Did they tell you to bring anything?*

Mariah Wind can't wait to be in the spotlight.

MARIAH: Just what I'm gonna wear in it. That's about it. I already had my makeup on. I had my hair already done.

ANA: *What time did you get there?*

MARIAH: About 4pm.

ANA: *What time did they start shooting?*

MARIAH: Around 4:30 or 5.

ANA: *So you didn't have to wait around that long.*

MARIAH: Well, they didn't start filming because they were taking the boxcover stills.

ANA: *And they treated you nicely?*

MARIAH: Oh yeah. I had a really nice time mostly because they were really cool people, and they respected me and I gave them that respect back.

ANA: *How many people were at this shoot?*

MARIAH: It was in this house and there was the cameraman, and Howard, the director, and John, the guy I was with. There were two other guys hanging out in the living room, but I don't know what they were there for.

ANA: *What did they explain to you when you got there?*

MARIAH: They told me I was going to do a blow job and then a full-on scene with John. I was going to talk to the camera, too. Howard was behind the camera as if he was the people watching it, you know? So he was asking me questions and I was just answering him and then little by little he talked me out of my clothes—I had on this little black tube top and this little black skirt—and then John came in and we did the scene.

ANA: *What kind of questions did Howard ask you?*

MARIAH: Just where I was from and what I did and what would I like to do.

ANA: *What did you say to John before you guys did your scene?*

MARIAH: I said hi to him, but that was it. We shook hands.

ANA: *It doesn't sound very complicated. Very businesslike.*

MARIAH: Mm-hm.

ANA: *What was the sex like? Did you enjoy it?*

MARIAH: Ummm. I don't think I'm going to "enjoy" any of this only because it's too fast for me. Because I'm more of a romantic and this is too fast for me. So I had to fake it all.

ANA: *How do you think you did?*

MARIAH: I think I did pretty good. I wasn't nervous at all. [Howard] wanted me to talk to the camera like I was having phone sex, so that's what I did. I slipped into character. They picked a really good guy to start me off with.

ANA: *So the guy came?*

MARIAH: Yeah. I want condoms in my videos so he had to quick take off his condom and then he came—not on my face but kind of by my chin, you know?

ANA: *Did you specify that you didn't want cum shots in the face?*

MARIAH: Yeah, I told them I didn't want it on my face.

ANA: *They didn't try to make you do anything you didn't want to do?*

MARIAH: No.

ANA: *How long did the whole thing take?*

MARIAH: I left around seven. So about three hours.

ANA: *Did everybody clap when you were done?*

MARIAH: No. *[Laughs]* But I got the cameraman's number! I was trying to get him in front of the camera, but he was too shy. It was really funny, because I was actually kidding around, I was like, 'Well I want the cameraman to come here!' So they had to stop filming because they were laughing so hard. Howard even took me out to eat afterwards.

ANA: *Are you happy with your first scene?*

MARIAH: Yeah! I'm really happy! I think this is going to be really fun. On Thursday, I'm doing a shoot that I think involves a blowjob—but they're also going to do this thing where I have my fantasy fulfilled, they're gonna do whatever my fantasy is. So I've been thinking of different things, what I want to do and things like that.

ANA: *So it's your second shoot and you are already involved in the creative part of making movies, huh?*

MARIAH: Yeah.

ANA: *What are you thinking of doing?*

MARIAH: There are different things I want to do. At first, I told them that I had always wanted to do it on the beach, but they told me it was summertime and there'd be too many people down there. Then I told them there's a place in the mountains where three waterfalls sort of come together, so they're thinking about going up there and filming something. I was also thinking about driving on a deserted road—that way my car could be in the video! *[Laughs]* And I requested that Jack Frost be in it. It's Temptress's brother. They called him and told him I requested him.

ANA: *Why did you request Jack Frost?*

MARIAH: Because I like him. *[Giggles]* I heard him mention that he was in the Marines and I like Marines, so I was thinking about having him in his Marine uniform and maybe having my car break down in the middle of the road, and he comes along to help me.

ANA: *Sounds good to me. Anybody else you'd like to work with?*

MARIAH: I don't know anybody else. There was this other guy I was supposed to do a blowjob with today, but I had to come home to pick up my daughter by six so I couldn't do it with him. So I had to cancel.

ANA: *Is there anything you know now that you didn't know on Friday—before you did your first sex scene?*

MARIAH: Bill told me: "The day you come home and say it was work, then that's the day you should just quit—because it should be all fun." To me, that first time was like work. It is fun at the same time, but to me it's work.

2

The Biz

(AS IN: "HOW DOES IT WORK?")

"I never got paid to kiss. I got paid to fuck."
—*Jerry Butler, adult film actor*

"Porn stars don't get paid to fuck. They get paid to wait."
—*Christie Lake, adult film actress*

Although cities like New York and San Francisco have given us plenty of porn in their heydays, if you are serious about being a sex performer, you will probably want to move to Los Angeles. Not only are 50 of the 85 top porn companies based there, but the City of Angels really lives up to it name: L.A. is home to the largest congregation of porn stars on Earth—around 1,600 of them!

The heart of the porn business is in the San Fernando Valley area of Los Angeles, often referred to as "Silicone Valley" or the "Valley of Sin." Some of the hottest adult spots in the Valley include Sherman Oaks, Canoga Park, Van Nuys, Studio City, and Chatsworth. Porn moved out to L.A. from New York in the mid-80s during the explosion of the home-video market. The reason was more financial than anything else, since rent, equipment, and talent were significantly cheaper there. Now, the Valley accounts for 90% of America's porn production. While mainstream film shooting in L.A. has decreased 13%, porn film production is up almost 25%. In July of 1999, one out of every five shoots in L.A. was an adult-film shoot. According to *Adult Video News*, the industry released 10,000 titles in 1999, up from 8,950 titles in 1998, and up from around 8,000 in 1996. That's adding nearly 1,000 new titles every year!

Considering that Hollywood only puts out about 400 theatrical releases a year, you can understand why people, whether they want to be talent or crew, have little difficulty finding employment in the adult industry. Porn taps into the underemployed, disaffected people who can't find—or are waiting for—work in the big Hollywood studios. "This summer, grips, gaffers and best boys of mainstream movie-making are marching down Hollywood Boulevard in an effort to save their jobs," the *L.A. Times* wrote. "But in the Valley... stagehands willing to stretch a boom over a couple in bed have zero problem finding work." The L.A. County Economic Development Corporation estimates the number of jobs created by the adult film industry is between 10,000 and 20,000. A sign of the times for porn's triumph over Hollywood came when Ron Jeremy, perhaps the only male porn star who is a household name in America, was invited to speak to executives at Paramount Pictures and Columbia Tri-Star on the theme, "Why can the porno industry spin out films for $50,000 in 3 days and make big profits while the major studios spend $40 million in six months and can't?" (Ron's answer? "Low overhead.")

The purpose of this following chapter is to explain what will be expected of you as an on-camera sex performer, as well as to debunk the myths that plague stars of adult film. Few people truly understand the effort and complexity that goes into capturing sex on film. After this Chapter, you will.

A. THE HIREARCHY

In *The Big Bad Book of Sex Opportunities for Men and Women*, I wrote: "Since the 60s, women have steadily become more and more interested in exploring adult entertainment. It's no longer a source of embarrassment or something they need to hide. Many of them routinely rent adult videos, go to strip clubs and even hire male escorts when they travel out of town. As a result, in some cities, the demand for male adult performers is growing even faster than the demand for female performers."

Of course, both men and women face excellent employment prospects if they are diligent and sincere. But as you have probably gathered by now, the Circus of X can be a radically different experience for male performers, who often make less money, and the female performers, who typically have shorter careers. While the preceding chapter mapped out the emotional tools you will need to be an adult sex performer, the following section maps out the physical tools you will need to be a talent in X. The sections are divided into "The Leading Lords" and "The Leading Ladies" so that we can focus on the differing requirements for men and women. But as the business stands today, both sexes start off pretty much the same way.

Agents. Just like in mainstream Hollywood, talent agents are the primary gatekeepers for porn. They can get you gigs with adult magazines, strip clubs, amateur video companies, and most importantly, the big production studios like Vivid, Wicked and VCA. The difference is that there are only a few agencies that matter in porn, so if you decide to approach them, make sure you are ready (i.e., that you've carefully read this book). If you blow it with the established agencies, you will have to go to the less scrupulous guys with bad toupees, cigarette-and-coffee breath and roamin' hands. The two biggest agencies—and the only two that have state-agency licenses to deal in X-rated films—are *World Modeling Agency,* run by Jim South, and *Reb's Pretty Girl International,* run by Reb Sawitz. (See the Appendix for a list of adult talent agents and their locations.)

Jim South gets on the horn and books another gig.

Jim South is the best known of all the L.A. agents. His World Modeling Agency has occupied the same building on Van Nuys Boulevard for 21 of the 25 years he has spent collecting talent—and he has handled virtually all the big names over that same period of time. Jim has been described as "smooth" and "slick," but when I met the man he had the appearance and demeanor of a soft-spoken, wily Texas rancher. Sporting a black pompadour with every hair in place and a small moustache, the 50-something South wears spit-polished black cowboy boots with dark blue jeans and short-sleeved shirts. Like any Texan, his belt buckles *are* as big as your head, but Jim is not an intimidating guy. He's no idiot—how do you think he has managed to stay on top for a quarter of a century? He has seen every scam, every grift, every dodge, every snake in the grass. If he senses you are nervous or apprehensive—as he says a good part of the ladies and gentlemen who come to see him are—he will joke with you, allay your doubts and fears. He will make you comfortable immediately upon meeting him. Like Bill Margold, whose P.A.W. counseling service is right down the hall from World Modeling, Jim can be a fatherly guide through the physical and psychological mine fields of porn.

I haven't met Reb Sawitz from Pretty Girl, but he entered the porn business nearly 30 years ago when he was still part of a motorcycle gang. Reb has discovered some true gems of the industry: Danyel Cheeks, Amber Lynn and the immensely popular Nikki Dial. He protects his girls—he used to go searching for filmmakers and other scumbags who didn't pay his starlets. Like his friend Bill Margold, who helped run Pretty Girl for a time (and helped cast most of the porn films between 1973 and 1982), Reb asks his visitors questions like, "What kind of work have you done? What do you want to do? What do you *not* want to do?" Then he will say something like, "You know, you could also make $500-$1,000 dollars a day doing movies."

Agents like Jim and Reb place ads in over 20 newspapers such as the *Orange County Register*, the *Simi Valley Star*, the *L.A. Weekly* and the *Ventura Star*. Jim used to hold monthly "casting calls" where potential talent would come down to his office and meet up with the big directors of X, like Henri Pachard, Max Hardcore, Joey Silvera, Ron Jeremy, Sean Michaels, Ona Zee and many more. Now he sees people by appointment only. He receives about 30 to 40 calls a day from potential clients. Jim explains to them clearly and with no crap what service he provides and what is available to prospective models and performers. He estimates that about half of the people who call him actually show up in person. If you decide to be one of them, you need not bring any resume or any portfolio—although having the latter, especially an amateur tape of you and a partner performing on-camera, couldn't hurt. What you absolutely MUST bring with you is two forms of identification that prove you are 18 years of age or older, which Jim photocopies and keeps in a file. If you don't come with the two forms of I.D., Jim won't even interview you.

Assuming you pass this test, he will sit you down and tell you the options available as an adult performer: Mainly, modeling for soft- and hardcore magazines and R- and X-rated films. He then will explain the pay arrangements and scales for different kinds of adult work. While we will discuss the fees that men and women make in their respective chapters, here is an approximate breakdown of the money paid for still photograph modeling for adult magazines:

Full Day (7 hours max): $250-$350
Half Day (1 to 4 hours): $125-$150
Playboy *Cable TV: $100-$150 (extra); $200-$300 (lead)*
Penthouse*: $1,000-$5,000*
Hustler *(1 to 2 days): $500 (guaranteed);*
$700-$2,000 (if pictures are used); Cover is an additional $500.

The female performer can often set her own prices, though generally speaking, newcummers are not in a strong negotiating position. On the other hand, talent no-shows on the set run as high as 25%, so new performers who show promptness, patience and some measure of responsibility might show up to a shoot and get paid more than was originally planned. Some companies will even pay a premium for first-timers, especially the women. The high rate of no shows is also good for you as far as getting on-camera "exposure." Jim's clients will often call him and say "so-and-so just canceled" and Jim will send over another actor or actress. And that could be you! You might also try to approach the agencies in the summer time, when most performers are more liable to be at the beach than on the set.

After the money business, Jim or one of his staff will take a standing, nude Polaroid of you. Jim says he signs about six clients a day. When they do sign, they specify what they will and will not do—oral, anal, girl-girl, group sex, D.P.s, gay, bi, that sort of thing. Females can list what men they will or will not work with. The information in the performer's file is updated as the performers extend their limits. The producers or directors come down to Jim's office and look through his portfolios of talent. If they choose you, they will contact you based on the information Jim provides for them in your file. You and the client will meet and exchange your phone numbers and go from there. All male and female performers are required to provide a photocopy of their AIDS tests before they show up on the set, and all performers are required to sign model release forms, which constitute your legal permission to put your image into mass circulation.

You can get an AIDS test anywhere. The most popular clinic is Sharon "Mitch" Mitchell's Adult Industry Medical Healthcare Foundation (AIM), which offers testing and counseling especially for adult performers. (For a more detailed description of AIM, see Chapter 3.) An AIDS test can cost anywhere from $35 to $50 to $95 and up. The preferred testing is the PCR/DNA test, which can catch the onslaught of AIDS/HIV infection much quicker and sooner than the old Elisa way of testing (also see Chapter 3), which only diagnoses the disease well after it has taken hold in an infected body.

It helps to have a little know-how in negotiating and marketing yourself, since Jim and his ilk are different from "regular" agents in that they don't manage their clients' careers. As I wrote in the *Big Bad Book*, "Women should not feel timid in bragging about their measurements to potential employers. And men, if you really do have 10-inch cocks that can stay rock hard for hours at a time, by all means, tell the producers. Believe me, it'll be music to their ears." This is where couples have a leg up, too, as a savvy boyfriend can help in the negotiating and maybe even can get himself a shot on-camera, especially if the woman requests that she work with her lover or husband the first few times so she can "loosen up" to more adventurous sex roles.

A porn agent deviates from a regular Hollywood agent in that guys like Jim South are not traditional Tinseltown "ten percenters"—meaning they do not deduct a percentage commission on the negotiated sum. Jim charges a flat $60 fee per 24 hours and sends two bills to the filmmaker, the agent's fee and the performer's rate. Considering the fact that 10,000 new adult films are being made per year, each with multiple performers, it is safe to say that Jim is doing all right for himself. He also hooks up his clients with scripts, locations, editing facilities and liability insurance.

Not that his world is so easy: Jim has often been the target of vengeful harassment from irate parents, spouses, lawmen or disreputable pornographers. In 1987, both Jim and Reb were arrested by the Los Angeles Vice squad, and their agencies temporarily shut down. It seems a young 16-year old stripper named Nora Louise Kuzma had falsified her birth certificate when she responded to an ad placed by Reb in an L.A. newspaper. The girl already had her name picked out before she started making porno films from 1984 to 1986: "Traci Lords."

Both Jim and Reb have been accused of supplying innocent, scared girls to hardcore pornographers like John T. Bone or Max Hardcore. (Reb claims he won't work with guys like that.) Jim has told the media that he has a "strict no dating policy" and does not socialize with his talent. Like Bill Margold, he maintains that would be "taking advantage" of his position if he were to date clients. Some people complain that Jim inhibits the careers of those he doesn't like. For example, he reportedly forbid producers from using actor Mike Horner because the two have been feuding for years. Jim has also been accused of billing clients for performers he didn't solicit. He has even been accused of trying to take over HIV testing, when male performers who showed up on the set with their HIV results from independent agencies were told they needed to get a test from South's nurse, at $130 a pop.

No doubt, Jim South has had his share of scandals—the Traci Lords under-age fiasco for one—which is why he requires TWO forms of identification. Then there was the 1985 documentary *Fallen Angels*, co-produced by Greg Dark of the legendary porn duo the Dark Brothers, which portrayed Jim as a "shifty salesman." Whether or not you will trust Jim or any other agent is a decision only you can make. If you are serious, your best bet is to schedule an appointment and meet the agents in person, as there is no substitute for face-to-face contact when assessing character.

If you prefer to avoid the agency route, you can always try to break into the business by contacting producers directly. While the older established companies rarely scout for talent, up-and-coming producers like Jill Kelly have been known to hire new performers. (See the Appendix for a list of porn producers.) Eden Rae Entertainment, owned by ex-porn star Eden Rae, is a fairly unusual production company in that it represents models, porn stars and feature dancers. Eden's requirements for prospective talent are a bit more strict than most agents, but they offer a good overview of what will be expected of you:

> *Our accepting male talent is not contingent on them having a woman to go into show biz with them. We only accept the best looking males and females, so we turn down a lot of them. We have a satellite office in California now, however... we maintain all record keeping at the main office with only duplicates on file here. We do not charge a flat fee, instead taking a 10% cut from the performer's pay. We require more stringent testing than other agents/companies. Hepatitis screenings are required every 30 days, hepatitis shots are required, PCR/DNA tests are required as per industry specifications. We will not accept anyone who does escort or massage parlor work. We turn down anyone with a drug conviction within the last 5 years; if over 5 years, we review it case-by-case. Any sexual-crime convictions will disqualify talent. Talent must not use drugs or alcohol on sets or other bookings, the only exception being featured dancers provided they drink in moderation, and responsibly. We will cancel all a performer's bookings and drop them [from the talent roster] should we find they are escorting, using drugs/alcohol on bookings, or are convicted of sex crimes or drug charges. We will also notify the company or person they were booking with why they are being dropped and booking cancelled. This will prevent companies from saying they didn't know he/she was escorting should anyone come down with diseases or whatnot.*

Let's hope there will be more agencies like Eden Rae Entertainment in the future. In the meantime, director Gary Sage offers this cautionary tale about how to tell if a porn "agent" is for real or not:

GARY SAGE: *Some of the* [Amateur productions] *might scout at strip clubs or conventions, but the large producers don't scout—I mean, girls can be approached by anybody saying, 'You wanna be in a porno movie?' who isn't necessarily even a producer of a porno movie. As far as I know, the Ed Powers or the Randy Wests of the world do not go to strip clubs scouting for new talent. They call Jim South and they say, 'Jim, who's new this week?' Most people will not scout. There's a few lower rung guys who call themselves agents who just want to fuck girls. First thing I would tell anybody going into an interview: You don't have to have sex with anybody to get a job. That's not necessary. There is no such thing as a casting couch. If they promise to get you a job because you're going to have sex with them, don't believe it. It's just like Hollywood. Yeah, sure there are some isolated cases where a casting couch might work, but in most cases it's not necessary and probably not recommended. If an agent tells you that you should have sex with him to prove how serious you are about getting into the Industry or have sex with him so he can see what you are like as a performer, that's bullshit. You shouldn't be dealing with that agent at all!*

Choosing Your Name. In Chapter 1, we discussed some reasons why everyone from the stars to the directors to the editors and production assistants choose false names when they work in porn. For example, journalist and TV writer Jerry Stahl wrote *Café Flesh*, one of the most influential porn films of the last 20 years, under the name F.X. Pope. Everyone has his or her own agenda, but what most people underestimate is the importance of choosing the right *nom de poon*—it's the difference between a rock group calling themselves *The Who* versus calling themselves *Root Boy Slim and the Sex Change Band.*

Another great example of the significance of choosing a name was demonstrated by one young "Eddie Adams from Torrance" (Mark Wahlberg) in *Boogie Nights*: If you saw the movie, you'll recall that Eddie came up with his stage name by closing his eyes and imagining a "bright blue neon light with a purple outline" that contained the words, Dirk Diggler. The name was so important to Eddie that he conceived of it blowing up into bits and pieces while it was illuminated on the neon sign.

Of course, you can always change your name later, as a lot of stars work under different names. Mary Dougherty works under both Candy Samples and Candy Apples; legend Veronica Hart has also worked under her name Jane Hamilton and occasionally as Sarah-Jane Hamilton—but to stick to one name means you can build a following of fans, who might be confused if you appeared in various films under as many names.

Some performers use more than one pseudonym when they do different genres of porn films. A minority of porn talent use their real names, among them Janine Lindemulder and John Stagliano. Many more drop their last name and just use their middle names, like Ron Jeremy and Tammi Ann. Some stars keep parts of their name or spin off variations, and some just have fun. For instance, Jerry Butler took his name from the 60s soul singer of the same name.

Many serious porn stars copyright their stage names. You can see ample evidence of this if you look up names in the Los Angeles County's Registry of Fictitious Business Names. If you still have difficulty choosing a name, Bill Margold is always a good guy to consult—although his choices sometimes lean a little too close to his own tastes for cheesy Hollywood musicals. ("Mariah Wind" he got from the song "They Call the Wind Mariah" from Lerner & Lowe's *Paint Your Wagon.*) Or log onto cybergossip Luke Ford's website (www.lukeford.com) and check out his list of real porn star names to get a feel for the different ways you can remake yourself.

B. THE LEADING LORDS

A 1994 *New Yorker* study reported that "36% of men age 18 to 24 had no sex with a partner in the past year," so you can see why the supply of guys willing to fuck for the camera is quite plentiful. Admit it, since you were an adolescent boy you've probably had fantasies about getting paid to bone a roomful of hot babes. What red blooded American male hasn't dreamt of this? But it is the few, the proud, who can do it professionally.

You'd better be sure you can handle yourself under bright lights with lots of people watching. You'd better be able to get a hard-on at will under even the most adverse conditions, as well as be able to deliver what is known as the "cum shot," the "pop shot" or, most tellingly, the "money shot"—and not when you want to, but when the directors *tell* you.

Men are valued primarily for their ability to perform on cue like this, a talent displayed at its highest level by perhaps only a dozen men in the jizz bizz today, including T.T. Boy, Peter North, Alex Sanders, Tom Byron, Steven St. Croix, Jon Dough, Dave Hardman, Joey Silvera, Rocco Siffredi, Chuck Martino, Jake Steed, Randy West, Bobby Vitale and Vince Voyeur. What many of them have to show for it is over 1,000 hardcore films in which they do a variety of exquisitely nasty things to an equal amount of beautiful young women. John Holmes once bragged that he slept with over 3,000 women in his life.

Getting In the Door. As a male performer in porn, the first thing to understand is that your role is decidedly secondary. With the exception of gay or bisexual films, the female is virtually 100% of the selling package in porn. It is the girls who will appear on the box covers; it is the girls who will get the focus of the credit sequences—luxurious shots with their names underneath—while you will be lumped in at the end of the credits with the other studmeisters. Not that the best woodsmen in the business care that much about recognition. The best are the best because they take control but remain detached at the same time when they are filming a sex scene.

Most men assume that they will have no problem performing for the camera. World Modeling's Jim South estimates that he gets up to 30 calls a day from men wanting to get a shot a performing. But whether that enthusiasm translates into on-screen "wood" is another story. More often than not, a male who has never experienced the harsh conditions of onscreen sex will not be able to "rise" to the occasion. Porn directors continually complain about the relatively small number of men in the business, but at the same time they are reluctant to try out new talent because so many men have performance anxiety, and directors don't want to waste precious film time.

For this reason, if you approach an agency, you should be ready to prove that you have what it takes. After all, no agent is going to risk making a fool of himself—he is only going to get you a job if he can personally guarantee that you will function. If you can demonstrate your skills when you register, whether in person or by a tape you bring in that shows you fucking a gorgeous babe, your chances of acceptance will go up astronomically. Porn star Annabel Chong suggests a trial run at home to make sure that you are not nervous in front of the camera. "A lot of people maybe after three to four shoots would eventually be very good performers," she emphasizes, "but it's the first two shoots that establish them as being good talent or just completely useless."

One good tactic is to make friends with a producer or director on a casual basis to get your first few jobs, and *then* register with an agency. For networking purposes, the X-Rated Industry has its little get-togethers (See "Industry Events" section of the Appendix). For instance, Bill Margold organizes a pickup football game at Coldwater Canyon on Saturdays. If you know who to kiss up to (reading this book will help), you can cultivate these people as friends. Tell them you admire their movies—although make sure you get their titles and directors right! They will think of you as a fan and be flattered.

Gary Sage has another suggestion: "The easiest way for a man to get into the Industry is with a woman. You bring her in and say that she will only work with you—initially. It might be a little bit harder to get work with those restrictions, but if she's a new girl, certain companies will want to hire you, especially if she's attractive. They'll want to hire her to be in their movies, and if she only works with one guy that's not that big of a deal. World Modeling doesn't care. Oftentimes the girls get to choose which men they will work with; if they haven't heard of you, they might not want to work with you. So it's kind of difficult. But then you get on a set, meet some girls, they get to know you and if they like you, they might want to work with you. Once they know that you can perform, you will get hired again. But if you just show up at a set and you don't belong there, you are not going to be accepted. If you can get yourself on by working with this one girl or whatever the situation is, then it's a lot easier. What this will do is allow you to prove yourself, it will allow you to actually do the scene, and if you can do the scene, word will get around. It's a small industry. Word gets around real fast. If you are able to perform you will get recommendations. So you have to get over that initial hurdle. Once you've done that, you don't have to work with the same girl anymore. You can work with any girl."

Bill Margold offers an alternative way to get a try out: the "fan fucks" perpetrated by enterprising women like Christi Lake and Nici Sterling. First, you join the club of the star who is hosting the "fan fuck." Then you can request an application form, fill it out, and mail it back with a photo of yourself. Anybody is eligible to write in, not just the good-looking guys. But it helps if you have a good idea or fantasy to suggest. To date, no man has broken into the adult film industry through a fan fuck, but it might be a good way to test you skill and resolve on camera. Be forewarned, though, as both Sterling and Lake will put your scene on their tapes even if you didn't get it up.

The final way into the world of X can also be the most exciting and rewarding—simply hire your own talent and make your own porn film. For more information on this option, see the 'Making Your Own' section of this chapter.

Your Essential Function. Simply put, the men in hardcore films are props for the female performers. You become a walking bodily function—a life support system for a cock. If this sounds a bit harsh, remember two things: (a) this is a *business*, it's *work* for your cock; and (2) professional detachment is actually a healthy attitude that will carry you a long way. According to porn legend Randy West, a male porn actor is a lot like a professional baseball player—namely because every would-be stud who's seen a porn film thinks he can bring home the (ahem) bacon. But as Randy explained to me, being a porn star can even be more demanding than a pro athlete.

RANDY WEST: *It's not as easy as it looks. A lot of guys see the movies and think they can all do it, but once you're on camera you've got to really know how to focus on what you're doing. You've got to block out all that's going on around you and just concentrate on the girl—and there's only so many guys who can do that on a regular basis. You know, still maintain a little social life and not bug out on the bad lifestyle habits. They weed themselves out, definitely. If you can't be counted on every time you show up for work, you're going to be out of the business soon. You've got to be 'on' at least nineteen out of twenty times—if you do one good and one bad and one good and one bad—that's going to be about it for you. In baseball they've got to bat .300 to be good; we've got to bat about .950 to be good. Otherwise, people don't spend money to waste the time. If you can't take care of business right away, they don't want to use you. Myself? I just love pussy and I just was able to concentrate on what I was doing and—you know, it's just one of those things. Sure, you can go try out for the Dodgers, but there's no guarantee you'll make the Dodgers.*

Randy West does a little flexing for the crowd.

The Littlest Crew Member. "Undoubtedly the most-asked question by the men who come to me for advice is, 'How Big Does my Dick Have To Be?'" says Bill Margold. A lot of factors come into play here: your build, height and weight all affect the way your member comes off on-camera. Bill suggests you look at your full erection from a few different angles—first in a mirror then on a video camera—to see how it looks. Then try this little test: make a fist around your Little Elvis with the head fully exposed for it to look good while being sucked on-camera. Your wang should be able to hit the back of an actresses throat if she indeed decides to deep throat you. When clothed, it wouldn't hurt if your dick made your pants bulge a bit. Wearing tighter pants or stuffing a sock down there is pointless, since it's all going to come off anyway!

On the other hand, cocks can be too big. Many female performers prefer medium-sized cocks so they won't get stretched out. John "The King" Holmes often couldn't get his fourteen-incher fully hard. Certainly, your dick should look good standing at attention. The preferred cock sticks either straight up like Vince Voyeur's or Randy West's, or it curves at an angle in an interesting way like T.T. Boy's or Marc Wallice's. Other examples of good porn cocks are Peter North, Rocco Siffredi, Jon Dough and Joey Silvera. Size can compensate for other shortcomings. Jamie Gillis wasn't a particularly good-looking porn actor, but he had an interesting dick and knew how to wield it. Jerry Butler wasn't known for his size, but he went all out with his acting and poured his heart and soul into his sex. Sean Michaels, the top black male performer in the industry, had a vasectomy before he started his porn career that cuts down on the power of his pop shots, but he makes up for it with his prodigious size. Ron Jeremy, porn's favorite son, is not considered the best-looking man in the industry, but he is known for his tremendous muscle control.

No question about it, your dick is one of your main selling tools (pun intended). Actor Steven St. Croix, one of the few men to be signed to a contract with Vivid, had his prick insured by Lloyd's of London. Alex Sanders is known for slapping his dick. Peter "The Painter" North is world famous for his huge cum shots, which can be up to seven to nine huge spurts of jizz that literally drenches an actress's face, butt, stomach, thighs and anything within a fifteen foot radius. (Pity the crew members.) The real elite woodsman also can stand in as a "stunt penis" for $50 to $100 bucks a scene (depending on the situation at hand), in case a younger or more inexperienced performer can't make wood. If, after all this, you are concerned that Mr. Wing-Wang doesn't match up, you can always shave your pubic hair. It tends to make your cock look larger on camera. Though most evidence suggests they don't work, you might also consider using vascular pumps to, shall we say, "beef" yourself up.

Attitude. A true woodsman doesn't focus on recognition as much as performance. By this, I don't mean your capacity to act like an asshole (unless your role on-camera calls for it) or to treat the women you perform with like trash. As we've seen, part of a male performer's job is to be in control, and this can start even before you and your partner film your scene. T.T. Boy is an actor who expertly slips into his aggressive-guy 'act' even before he makes it to the set—although, he's sometimes not as popular amongst actresses because he has a tough time slipping *out* of character. The persona you adapt, which we will discuss in a bit, can help you become a better actor (i.e. reader of lines) and can help you get into character more easily. Professionalism counts here: if you are asked to do something by a director, do it. If an actress wants you to be more gentle, slow down. Keep the complaining to a minimum—leave that to the diva actresses. While bonding often occurs between male performers, competition is still stiff amongst them, so make as few enemies as possible. If you establish a reputation for friendliness, promptness, and reliability, you will get more work than you can handle, as you will see in my interview with Guy DeSilva. Attitude also applies to your ability to get it up and keep it up for up to two hours of shooting time. Again, taking your acting seriously but not taking the sex *that* seriously is the fine line any male performer must walk.

Stalwart woodsman Jon Dough is the perfect example of this right attitude. Even before he became one of Vivid's few "contract woodsmen," Jon was working as much as 25 days a month, making love to a different woman every day. One important reason why is that he doesn't over-intellectualize or try to make a statement. He just does what he does, almost like a Zen Buddhist.

Other Functions. Says porn director Gary Sage: "The one thing a director looks for in male talent is, for lack of a better word, 'control.' As directors, we give the actors certain guidance during the sex scenes, but for the most part the female talent take their cues and directions from the male talent, as it is in most sexual situations. So a guy that's simply pumping away is not interesting. A guy who takes command of the situation and gets the girl to do things that she wants to do, to excite the girl, that's what we call 'giving a good performance.' The absolute minimum is to show up on-set and get your dick hard. But you have to be able to excite the girl and put her in a number of different positions. You have to do whatever you have to do. You basically have to go through the motions of being a good sex partner. This is why you see the same male performers again and again. They don't just have big dick and fuck hard; they put themselves in tune with how the woman is feeling. It's chemistry between a man and a woman—that's why certain scenes are 'hot.' That's why you see certain scenes when it looks like the two people are fucking and actually enjoying each other, and then some scenes are like, 'Yeah they're going through the mechanics of it, but it's not really exciting.' It's like a medical or educational film. It might as well be two monkeys or two water buffalos. In some cases it practically is.

"One of the most important things you have to keep in mind when you are having sex on film is that you are playing to the camera—even more so than you are playing to your partner. As the male talent, it is your responsibility to show off the girl. Plus you have to be aware of where the camera is. If you put your hands in front of the camera and they can't see the penetration, you are not doing your job. Sometimes you will hear things like the Director going, 'I'm on your face; I need more emotion on your face' or 'I need something more from you guys to make it look a little hotter.' So you have to be able to do that. Believe it or not there is some actual acting involved. If you are a really vocal, outgoing, exhibitionistic kind of person who loves sex, you won't have to do that so much. But if you are generally quieter or much more sedate when you're having sex, you have to put on a bit of a show. Male talent can take on different styles. There are men who are more aggressive, guys that are louder, or whatever. For females, you don't have to be screaming till the high heavens like some girls do, but you might have to be a little more vocal. Some scenes might even require that you talk dirty."

So you see, the verbal and mental play an important role in porn. But what do you do if you don't find your leading lady that attractive or if she isn't that into the sex? Or what if she is a bit of a drunk or a diva, constantly stopping filming for a cigarette, a glass of water or to touch-up her makeup? Many actors and actresses will look at attractive crew members—who are always clothed and sort of forbidden fruit—to goose their imaginations. You might also want to keep some sexy fantasies floating in the back of your mind to replay when needed.

Another strategy is to move the female into a more gratifying position. Probably the easiest active role for a man is giving oral cunnilingus. The easiest passive one is to receive fellatio. The hardest scenes to shoot are the scenes with more than one man, which means more than one dick. ("It's like playing twister with an octopus," says Maestro Margold.) Many men are squeamish about even the thought of their balls slapping up against another man's leg. Chances are, though, if you refuse to participate in group sex or gang bangs because of this, you probably shouldn't be fucking for a living. It could also cut down on your ability to get hired for future roles.

What to Bring to the Set. Bill Margold advises young studs: "Come prepared to play a variety of roles. This means shave, (unless you have been specifically told not to or if you were supposed to grow a beard for a role), shower, and bring a selection of wardrobes—at least a suit, casual outfit, and an alternative outfit in case they hate everything else." Forget clothes with logos on them because of the copyright problems. Remember that certain colors like black, red and white clothing will cause an instantaneous dissension, so don't bright those colors unless they ask you. If you like a certain lubricant, bring it. It's not a bad idea to bring your own towel, soap and various other toiletries. Also, if you have a pager or a cell phone, turn it off while you film, as the noise it makes could ruin a scene. Also remember to bring your own water. Because of AIDS and other sexually-transmitted diseases (STDs), you should also bring your own condoms. Many times the bigger companies will provide condoms on set, but they might not be what your cock likes or is used to. Some women have allergic reactions to certain brands of condoms, so many of the actresses will provide their favorite kind for you. There are rubbers being manufactured now that are made out of thin goatskin for maximum sensation; there is also a rubber called "Crown" that is so thin it cannot be picked up on camera. If you keep your pubic hair well-groomed but not shaved, then the hair around the base of your dick will help to keep the condom hidden. Some male stars lightly perfume their private parts despite the fact that it stings.

Pacing Yourself. Because being a porn stud is a demanding job, it can cause males to lose some of their interest in sex. This is especially true since the male organ can only perform so much in a 12 to 14-hour shoot period. "How many times a male porn actor can get an erection per day is up to him—at most I would say twice," director Gary Sage told me. "Most producers would not schedule a male performer to do more than two on-screen orgasms, or scenes, a day. That's pretty much the maximum."

A lot of the men in the Industry brag about being able to get it up and cum on cue up to five or six times a day. This is very rare. In most cases, to overuse your cock is to result in very bad cum shot—your ejaculate won't be as white or thick and won't show up as anything impressive on your leading lady's face or on camera. Also, the urethra is very sensitive and will weaken when it is used too much. This is why it may be wise to consider your porn career as more of a side thing to your "regular" professional pursuits. It's tempting to become dependent on the Industry to the point where you want to work 25 out of 30 days of the month, but unless you are a major stud, your dick will protest.

Your Pop Shot. Over time, the cum shot has evolved to marking the proper end of any sex scene, mainly because it proves that the sex you just saw was "real." Scenes that don't have the cum shot feel constipated, unconsummated, unfinished. It is less important to deliver a big pop shot than to deliver one at all. "There's no, 'Oh, I'm not done yet, gimme a little more' or 'Oh, I'm going to cum now,'" says director Gary Sage. "You cum when the director tells you to cum. In the old days, you had to count down from ten because they were working on film; you couldn't just stand there running thousands of feet of film waiting for some guy to cum because it's expensive. In the old days, they would build up to within ten or fifteen seconds of orgasm, count it down and then pop on cue. Now we have video so it's cheaper, but you still don't want to be sitting there for a half-an-hour waiting for this guy to pop because that's a half hour of your time. And time is money."

There is the rare occurrence—almost as rare as a hole-in-one in golf—of the mythic "double-pop shot," where a man cums twice in succession in the same minute. If this happens to you, it will be a plus for the scene and probably get you a lot of accolades and attention. But don't "overact" for your cum shot—definitely look like you are having the time of your life, but don't go into over-exaggerated facial contortions or anything. A lot of the time directors will shoot your facial reactions separately from your real orgasm, but the overact rule still applies. "If they want the reaction shots of your cum shot, and you look like you're taking a shit" says Bill Margold, "the vision is destroyed." Cum shots are necessary to a scene, but your popularity will not hinge on how much. Actors Herschel Savage and Randy West have had long-standing and lucrative porn careers despite their lack of copious cum-loads. Marc Wallice has never really had big cum shots, but because of the arch of his dick it sprays across the girl's ass or face and looks quite interesting on-camera. Some great cummers include Peter North, Ron Hightower, Joey Silvera and Woody Long. Peter North admitted in an interview that he once hit a camera and the cameraman who was filming his cum scene. Now that's true woodsmanship!

Legendary woodsman Peter North has a secret recipe.

It is also important to footnote that your diet may affect how your spunk will taste in your co-starlet's mouth. Fried and spicy foods and heavy cholesterol diets make a man's cum taste salty. Most veterans recommend a diet of salads, fruits, and chicken. "I work out and play ice hockey; I try to eat 85% healthy," Peter North told me. "I have my days where I don't eat as healthy. I supplement my meals with Myoplex which is a protein drink—top notch, too; one of the best protein drinks out there right now. Three meals and two of those shakes."

Often people watch a cum shot and swear it was "faked"—which is ironic since the original purpose of showing a male orgasm onscreen was to prove that, "Yes! The sex really did happen!" For the most part, cum shots are only faked in dire circumstances—like when a stunt cock can't be found and no one's being paid overtime. Porn watchers often ask whether they use things like whipped egg whites or yogurt or hand cream to fake cum in movies. The answer is usually not in videos, but sometimes in still shoots or photo layouts. There you're only simulating sex, so there's no real cum shot. The most popular substitute for the real thing is Tame Crème Rinse.

Your Walk and Talk. Many porn actors have developed certain looks and personas—or certain stylish or visual hooks—to stand out from the platoons of walking penises. Tom Byron is the "rock 'n' roll guy" with the tattoos and his frequent appearance on box covers holding an electric guitar. Rocco Siffredi is the hot, horny "Italian guy who loves to fuck." Ron Jeremy is the clown, the comic—he will often improvise hilarious dialogue while he's performing with his Leading Ladies. Randy West is the California muscle-bound Greek god who also talks like a good ol' country boy—"a cross between Hercules and Opie" one journalist wrote. John Stagliano, who directs more than he acts, has his sensitive, horny, ass-loving alter ego "Buttman." Joey Silvera is quite good at playing drunken, down-and-outers who just happen to be tan and muscular. Steve Drake established himself as the "Tom Selleck of Smut," Bobby and Samantha Fox were "the Sonny and Cher" of porn, and Tony Montana was sort of like the Latin lover type, a cross between Desi Arnaz and a sleazier Ricky Martin. Even fiftysomething Dave Cummings carved out a niche for himself as the horny older guy who lives other middle aged men's fantasies of fucking P.Y.T.'s ("Pretty Young Things").

And then, of course, there is Peter North, who has carefully cultivated his hugely successful jock look. "Back when I started there weren't really many guys who were physically appealing to the women—you know, clean-cut, all American-type guys—so I kind of stood out in that respect, and that worked out for me," Peter told me. "I also tried to do the best job I could which I guess becomes easier if you have a number of different attributes that help you out. You may not be the best looking or have the best body or the biggest schlong, but maybe you have a package or even a 'gimmick'. I could remember lines pretty easily and my pop shot is sort of my trademark—it's why I'm famous. How I do it is a secret. When I retire I'm going to reveal how I did it. There's a lot of genetics involved, too."

Peter North has built his career, very much like Colonel Sanders, on keeping the recipe for his successful cum shots "secret." For porn, that's brilliant marketing!

Learning Your Lines. Always bring your script to the set. Even if you're not the greatest actor or line reader, it shows professionalism and respect for the people who hired you in the first place. Porn is perhaps the only entertainment industry where you can go into the set cold and pull off a half-decent performance. Your cock doesn't have to learn lines. Says Bill Margold: "Your hand is your best friend, second only to your dick. If you have a script, you are also responsible for your lines. Keep the dick interested while you learn your lines. If you blow your dialogue they can punch it in later. They can't do that with your cock."

Currently, actor Herschel Savage is the only known male porn star who can learn and recite lines while maintaining an erection at the same time. (Maybe you can be the next!)

Drugs. Don't do them. You will just be sabotaging yourself. Women may be able to mask the effects of something they snort or smoke beforehand, but you are the man and your role is a precarious balancing act between losing and maintaining your "control." Any drug you ingest before a scene could topple you off that wire—and the main evidence of that will be a penis that won't come out to play for the scene. Some porn actors smoke a little marijuana before they do a scene because pot is a stimulant and a relaxant at the same time, but cocaine is the Ebola Virus to woodsmen. It can quickly become a vicious circle—you do coke to deal with the pressure so you can get it up so you can make more money to buy more coke to deal with the pressure. If you're strung out, at least have the decency to stop working until you get clean. Mr. Schwantz will appreciate the break. If you show up on a set coked out of your skull, your mind might want to perform, but he might not.

Money. Harry Reems, now one of the legends of early porn, was reportedly paid a measly $100 for his role in the ground-breaking film *Deep Throat*, a film which was estimated to gross between $100-$600 million by the late eighties. Harry's co-star, Linda Lovelace, received $1,200. Such gender inequality is still common in porn. Almost without exception, leading male performers earn less money than the top females. (Ironically, Harry Reems was also the highest known paid actor in porn, receiving $75,000 for the film *Society Affairs*, where he bones twelve women—that's $6,250 per chick!) The average day rate of a male performer is $150-$600 per day and includes two pop shots. Even the guys who've been doing it for years commonly get $500. Still shoots can earn you from $50 to $200. Typically, male performers go by the day rate or set their rates based on the number of pop shots they are required to provide. Actors are often paid in cash, although the production manager may prefer to write you a check when the working day is done. Porn companies need to keep scrupulous records and writing checks makes the money easier to report to the Feds.

Unlike actors in mainstream entertainment, the average porn actor doesn't get overtime or residuals from the sales of films he appears in. This is true for women as well—although many do profit from independently marketing themselves. One actress, Vivid contract girl Ginger Lynn, managed to be savvy enough to negotiate a deal for a percentage of the royalties from her movies. (Oddly, no actor or actress had previously thought to do this.) Only recently has Vivid begun signing men to exclusive contracts. The rest of the bunch is left to compete for jobs or use new technologies to market their images, which I discuss later.

Straight, Bi, Gay. In the past, males who performed in the gay market found it difficult to cross over to heterosexual films. This, however, may be changing somewhat. Since porn is a drawing ground for people with diverse sexual tastes, it isn't uncommon that men, gay or not, appear in bisexual films in which they make love to other men as well as women. Many of these men use different names: Marc Wallice used the name "Don Weber," Eric Price was "Charlie Stone," and Joey Verducci was "Mac Reynolds." Numerous gay performers fuck straight women in bisexual porn, among them Chance Caldwell, Chris Dano, Dean Glass and Johan Paulik. Jeff Stryker in particular wasn't shunned but instead became one of the biggest male stars in all three genres. In fact, many straight porn women prefer working with men from gay porn because they feel the men tend to be better looking!

Of course, this creates significant problems with health and trust in a high-risk industry like porn films. Bill Margold advises men who are strictly interested in the gay market to skip the mainstream agencies and producers. The bi/gay market is a completely different business from straight porn, and it is generally made and distributed by companies that are exclusively devoted to that market. According to *Adult Video News*, which publishes a special edition for the gay porn market, the following are some of the top agencies and agents for gay porn: Entertainment (Joe Romero), Brad's Buddies (David Forest), Con Merten Agency, D&D Entertainment (Dan Byers), Falconi Men (Giorgio Falconi), Jump Start casting (Raul Rodriguez), Red Dragyn (Fred Dragyn), Show Boys Entertainment (Johnny Johnston), Southwest Management (Peter Scott), Sports Models USA (David Crowell), Steele Productions (Troy Steele) and Your Fantasy Productions (Johnny Rey).

C. PORN PROFILE: AN INTERVIEW WITH GUY DeSILVA

Comedian Chris Rock once made the crack: 'Everyone in that [porn] business is a 'porn star.' Aren't there any 'porn character actors'? He obviously hadn't met Guy DeSilva. Guy has carved out a lucrative and solid career as an able, responsible and dependable supporting actor. Born in New York, Guy is also half black; he explodes a lot of myths about the tendency of African-American men to not get hired or earn as much as the white-male porn performers. He gets paid well and has worked for practically all the big names in the business, like Vivid, Wicked and VCA. He is the consummate example of the professional porn stud who keeps his head and dick in separate worlds. At 43 years old he is still single.

Guy DeSilva is the ultimate professional.

ANA LORIA: *So I've always wanted to know: how do you keep from cumming when two gorgeous babes are slicking down your man-sword with their tongues?*

GUY DeSILVA: That's one hell of a first question. Actually, cumming too soon has never been one of my problems. It's only happened to me like three times in the six years I've been in this business. Most of the time the problem comes when I'm trying to *[have an orgasm]*. I can't explain it. It's from working so much, I guess. When you work so much, cumming becomes harder, believe it or not, instead of easier. When I started out it was much easier to cum, but when you stop-and-go and stop-and-go and stop-and-go that makes it much harder. If you're shooting Amateur or Gonzo stuff like John Stagliano they usually don't stop and you can get a good rhythm going. But shooting hardcore and softcore at the same time—man, that's *work*.

ANA: *How did you first get into the business? Did you first go see Jim South?*

GUY: No, it was actually through someone on the production crew. I was hesitant—I remember asking them if I could wear a wig or a fake moustache or something. My first scene was a three way with a woman and another guy. The other guy was Steven St. Croix.

ANA: *Wow! Pretty heavy company.*

GUY: That was actually one of his early films. The scene was okay. I was a little nervous.

ANA: *I bet. Especially since it was your first time. They didn't 'ease' you into it, like start with a jack-off scene or even just girl-guy?*

GUY: Nope. Right to it.

ANA: *How'd it go?*

GUY: It was a little weird. I just tried to ignore everything.

ANA: *Did you do anything mentally or physically to prepare for it?*

GUY: Just watched a lot of pornos. *[Laughs]* I've been a fan all my life. Actually, one of the reasons I wanted to get into this business was that I watched a lot of tapes by John "Buttman" Stagliano. I used to collect his stuff. I finally got to work with him, and when I told him this, he used it in the movie. You know, that's his style, that real informal, voyeuristic thing. It was called *Buttman's Inferno*. I just talked right into the camera to tell John and this other fellow named Tim Lake, 'Oh, I'm a huge fan of your movies.' And then the action, with us three and these two other girls—Krysti Lynn and another girl named Sheena—takes off from there.

ANA: *What was Stagliano like to work for?*

GUY: Oh, he was great. The best as far as I'm concerned because he doesn't like to stop. A lot of cameramen and directors will stop you a bunch of times because they want to shoot softcore or the box cover or this or that—and sometimes when you stop and go and stop and go, it's a lot more difficult. But [Stagliano] knows that. He might take maybe four stills during the whole shoot, and he also takes stills of the girl beforehand. But once he starts shooting, he doesn't like to stop. That's why he gets such good scenes. He doesn't even have crew with him when you shoot for him—no lighting, no crew, no one else on the set but him.

That's why he gets such good stuff, because there's no distractions. He's one of the easiest people to work for.

ANA: *Who else is good to work for?*

GUY: I worked for Max Hardcore. He's actually a soft-spoken guy. He has a reputation for being brutal with some of the girls, but you either like him or you don't. There's no in-between with Max Hardcore. I didn't have a problem with him. I mean, my style of working is not quite like his. He stays out of your way, but he also gets in there and engages you; he might want you to get a little rough, like himself. I worked for him twice. He really doesn't use a lot of guys; just himself a lot and maybe 2 other men.

ANA: *Do the majority of directors treat the male talent differently from the female talent?*

GUY: Sometimes, yes. They treat the male talent like props and cater to the female talent. Unlike Stagliano, who caters to the male talent; he makes sure you get 'teased', he makes sure you're comfortable. That has a lot to do with his product being so good.

ANA: *Who would you not work for?*

GUY: It's funny. I've said I wouldn't work with certain people and have ended up working for them anyway. And it didn't turn out so bad. Like I wasn't too crazy about working for Extreme, it's a new company. John T. Bone does stuff for Extreme, and I ended up working for him at least 15 or 16 times.

ANA: *He doesn't have a great reputation...*

GUY: I know, he doesn't. But I've never had any problems with him. Never. He never bounced a check on me, never disrespected me—I have nothing bad to say about him. But he is very direct, he tells you what he wants, he doesn't beat around the bush, and he shoots pretty extreme stuff, too.

ANA: *You mentioned you were an actor trying to break into mainstream films. How did your acting training prepare you for doing adult films?*

GUY: Just in preparation. Being on time, knowing what you need to do. Knowing what they're expecting from you. I try to find out all of those things before I even show up. But it's nowhere as extensive as regular movies. The biggest one I ever did was a film for Vivid called *Sin Sex*, which was a huge project with a big budget, shot on film. Paul Thomas produced it, and Michael Zen directed it. It was a period piece where I played a gangster from the 1940s. Everyone thought I was perfect for it. It was a good movie, too. They sent me my dialogue ahead of time—just as it should be, a lot of times you get your script as soon as you get there. That's why it comes off so bad sometimes. But they did it right, and I was prepared, they had wardrobe, the whole bit. I was real proud of that. I was sort of the new kid on the block among the other men in the movie, but I think I came off pretty good.

ANA: *Is there some sense of competition between the few men who do make it in porn?*

GUY: Generally speaking, I get along with guys as well as women. I'm not into competing against them—a lot of guys like to do that. They get into the business to compete with each other. I don't. I'm pretty well liked in the business. I get this 'nice guy' thing all the time. 'This is Guy, he's one of the nicest guys in the business.' I'm always getting that. I get along with people pretty well, so I don't have a problem. But there's always going to be somebody who doesn't like you for whatever reason.

ANA: *How is it different for the guys in porn as opposed to the women?*

GUY: It's more work for the men than the women, without a doubt. Psychologically it's heavy on the women. A lot of women have to take a little drink to loosen up. A lot of guys tend to smoke a little pot just to zone everything else out. But it's generally more different for men than for women, because men can't fake it and women can. It's gotta be real, and sometimes when you show up to a set you have that little before-scene stress, because you're wondering how you are going to do. But sometimes it's good when you're a little nervous.

ANA: *Everyone, I think is a little nervous before sex. Even when it's intimate.*

GUY: Exactly, so you can imagine how much more nervous you are before a camera and a bunch of people!

ANA: *What sort of techniques do you use to get you through a sex scene?*

GUY: The one I just mentioned: smoking a little pot. Other than that I basically try to block everything else out and focus on who I'm working with, on what I'm doing. It's all in the head, mainly. You can show up really horny and by the time you get to do the scene totally lose it, if you're not focused right.

ANA: *Are there any movies you did that you are particularly proud of?*

GUY: The *Buttman's Inferno* thing, definitely. A scene from that was nominated for 'Best Group Scene' [by *Adult Video News*].

ANA: *Do you have a lot of good friends in the Industry?*

GUY: Acquaintances. *[Laughs]* I make a lot of 'acquaintances' in the business. A lot of people call me their 'friend' more than I call them my 'friend.' I get that a lot, I'm not kidding. I'm not just stroking myself. People like to say that: 'Oh, Guy! He's one of my best friends!'

ANA: *Is that how you chose your porn name?*

GUY: No, actually, I figured when *[producers or directors]* call Jim South and say, 'We need guys!' I would pop right up in Jim's mind: 'Guys? Guy? Oh, Guy! Call up Guy DeSilva!' DeSilva was actually my mother's maiden name.

ANA: *Do you have a diet or exercise regimen that you put yourself on, especially when you are working a lot?*

GUY: I just try to eat a lot of pasta. I have to keep my weight up. I'm one of those people who lose quicker than I gain. Pasta's good for protein, tuna fish... I'm not the greatest eater or exerciser; luckily I have a high metabolism. I haven't worked out in over a year! In fact, that reminds me, I gotta get back into the gym.

ANA: *Did you ever smoke pot to do a scene, get the munchies during the scene, and go stuff yourself after the scene?*

GUY: *[Laughs]* Oh yeah, that's happened.

ANA: *What do you think is the biggest myth of the Industry?*

GUY: When people see the cut version *[of a sex scene]* they don't see all the things that happen in between, like guys losing their erections, or sometimes on camera guys actually look 'bigger' than they really are. Size doesn't always matter, sometimes girls will choose guys with smaller ones than bigger ones. Size does help when you're doing stills, though, because they want to see a lot and if you aren't as big, they don't see as much. So it helps in some ways and in other ways it doesn't.

ANA: *What did you think was the most inaccurate thing about the movie* Boogie Nights?

GUY: Not all porn stars fall from grace. There are some of them that make it into a good, successful business career. They didn't show that too much. It seemed like everyone was fucking up.

ANA: *Are men judged for the size of their 'pop shots'?*

GUY: Uh, yeah... but sometimes when you're working so much you don't always have a good one. But Peter North, I don't know what his trick is. He must have an abnormally large prostate gland or something. He's pretty amazing.

ANA: *What's Sean Michaels* [the biggest black director in the business] *like to work with?*

GUY: I worked for him last week, actually. Him and I have a lot of respect for each other. We're both the same in that we're both soft-spoken, well-mannered and...well, I'm not as 'cool' as Sean. Sean needs to spread some of the coolness around to other people. *[Laughs]* He keeps all the 'cool' for himself!

ANA: *What do you mean? You make him sound like Puff Daddy.*

GUY: I say that jokingly, of course. Sean and I were doing this scene with dialogue where we had to curse each other out. It was so odd the way we did it: he said 'fuck you, man' and then I said, 'no, fuck *you*, man.' We cursed each other out like two gentlemen. Instead of being angry, we were being civil to each other. This scene we just did the other day was awesome. We had this French girl named Gina Vise—a new girl—with a body just built for sex. I found her, and Sean found this other girl, a black girl, brand-new also—it ended up being one hell of a scene. *[Sean and I]* both were strong and in our prime, and the girl—man, this is no joke, before Sean even came into the scene she just grabbed me and put me inside her and here I am thinking I'm going at it vaginally. But I look down and it turns out I'm in her ass. I couldn't believe it. She was pushing me to go as hard as possible. Then Sean went in—and you know how long he is—and he just went in ALL THE WAY. It was a good scene. It's going to be talked about.

ANA: *You introduce new talent to directors like you did the French girl?*

GUY: I do, but I always tell the girl to mention who she's with. An agent, is what I mean. 'Cause I don't play agent, I just offer referrals. So I want to make that clear. I try to make sure I don't get in between the agent and his talent to make sure that the agent gets paid. Because agents getting cut out is a problem in this business, and then they get pissed at talent for doing the network thing and leaving them out of the loop. So you gotta be careful about that.

ANA: *Do you give the girls you bring in some sort of little 'speech' about what to expect?*

GUY: Yeah, I'll tell them what to expect from certain people. I'll tell them 'So-and-so is very professional, very particular about what he wants. He's not going to try to get a blowjob.'

ANA: *Does that last thing happen a lot?*

GUY: It happens a lot. Definitely. Especially if they're by themselves. There are a lot of producers who won't mess with the talent that way, but there are a lot of them that will. So, I'll just give them a little warning. Some girls don't mind, though; they're expecting it.

ANA: *Girls can often choose who they work with. Have women performers ever requested you personally?*

GUY: Oh yeah. I've been requested a few times by girls I don't even know. Just the other day this girl named 'Bronze' from Video Team requested me for a group thing. When I met she said, 'I've seen your stuff.' So it was a little flattering.

ANA: *Who are some of the bigger-name actresses you've worked with?*

GUY: Oh, let's see... Nina Hartley, Jeanna Fine, Celeste and J.R. Carrington all gave great scenes. One of my favorites is Johnni Black because she's really hot, and she doesn't just go through the motions. There's a few I want to work with, like Missy. Oh, there's a few others I can't think of right now.

ANA: *What was Nina like to work with?*

GUY: I was actually nervous with Nina, because we got intellectual with each other right before we did the scene. She got in my head, so when we started doing the scene it was weird. I wasn't at my best, and I'd been wanting to work with Nina for over 10 years! In fact, I kind of requested her. It was a film we shot for *['couples' porn director]* Candida Royale called *The Bridal Shower.* Candida told me Nina was going to be in the film and I told her, 'I'd love to work with her' and Candida put me with her. I was on the box cover and everything. But after we did the sex scene, Nina came up to me and said, 'Guy, when you looked down at me, you thought,

'Nina Hartley is giving me head,' didn't you?' I shouldn't have done that. I should have just enjoyed it and put all that other stuff out of my head. Mike Horner and Jonathan Morgan were also in it. I got the top billing too, which was pretty flattering.

ANA: *To what do you contribute the longevity of your career?*

GUY: Being reliable, showing up on time, being easy to get along with, and pulling off decent scenes. I have my days. I have times when it's just not happening. But I hang in there; I don't give up.

ANA: *What's the most you've ever worked per week or per month?*

GUY: How about a day? I worked four times in one day once—four different scenes for four different people. I was horny and I was testing myself. On the last one, I was pulling on it for almost an hour trying to cum. I mean, at home you can do it many times, but on a set it's quite different. After that day I treated myself to a beer and then went right to bed. I won't do that again. Dave Hardman is a guy who can get it up and cum six or seven times a day. No joke. The guy is an enigma. He was doing this before Viagra, too! I don't know how he does it.

ANA: *Did you ever try Viagra for a sex scene?*

GUY: I've tried it, but I don't like to depend on it. It does give you a hard-on, but it almost desensitizes you in a way. You're not as sensitive when you have sex on it.

ANA: *Does Viagra make it harder to cum?*

GUY: No, but I still don't like to depend on it. But, for instance, if I have three scenes in one day and I'm really busy and I'm real tired, I might try it. A lot of the newer guys coming into the business use Viagra and they still can't get it up. Why? Because they're not *performers*. After working so much sometimes your body just shuts down. That's why there are times when I'll screen my calls because I really don't want to work, and I really don't want to come up with an excuse. A lot of the time I'll just get back to them later, and it's already over with. I never thought I would turn down money and women at the same time. Those are the two things that most men are after! But there are times when you gotta do that and say 'no.' I never thought it'd come to that in my life.

ANA: *You mentioned earlier that you've tried to get out of the business a few times. Why are you still doing adult films?*

GUY: It's too hard to leave the business because there's too much money to be made.

ANA: *Even though men don't make as much money as women do?*

GUY: No they don't, but the men work more and have longer careers. So it balances itself out.

ANA: *Have you noticed any kind of social stigma associated with acting in porn?*

GUY: It's hard to date outside of the business. Like you have a girlfriend who's living with you, you leave the house, 'Honey, I'm going to work, I'll see you later.' It's kind of odd. It's also difficult to date people inside the business—that's one of the major drawbacks I think. It's kind of awkward. If you're secure with each other and you understand each other, you can work it out. I really don't date that much. I just don't. I used to work for Federal Express before I got into the industry. People didn't know what I did outside of work. Then one day, one of the employees brought in a magazine I was in. It went around the whole station, and I wasn't too happy about it. To him it was just a joke—he even apologized to me later—but it went around, and for weeks afterwards girls were giving me grins and things like that.

ANA: *Did you get any dates out of that?*

GUY: There was one woman who was interested, but I didn't go there. Eventually I got fired for something. They were nitpicking me at work, I don't know if it was related to them knowing about my modeling work or anything—but I ended up going over some heads and got my job back. That pissed a few people off, I think, because I won. When I came back I was really in the hot seat. So that's how it ended—even though there was a clause in my contract saying as long as I don't represent the company in any way it didn't really matter what I did. I still don't know if that was because of my 'other' job or not. I still don't feel I did anything wrong.

ANA: *What do you do when you have wood problems?*

GUY: I'll take a little break and get my focus together. I might even look at the make-up girl or something, just for visual stimulation. Or I look at another girl on the set that doesn't even perform. Sometimes that's enticing—because you can't have her. You gotta fill your mind with all kinds of stuff: either a scene you did the day before or something. You just search for something to stick in your head, and that's what works.

ANA: *So what's it like doing a double penetration?*

GUY: As long as you're comfortable with your sexuality and you don't have any phobias about working with men it can go well. But if you have problems slapping balls with another guy, the scene is going to have problems. D.P.'s are difficult work. If you're on the bottom, which means you're the one in the woman's pussy, you can get crushed. *[You]* can't move that much, and you can't get a rhythm—it can be hard to cum or keep your erection. Then you have to stop, get up, and go again. If you're on the top, meaning going into the woman's ass, they place the camera underneath you to catch the action. You have to keep your legs up, and that can get tiring. But they are shooting over you. You can keep both of your legs down and support yourself, keeping the blood flowing so your legs don't fall asleep. If you keep your legs up for too long it can affect your blood flow to certain areas and then you can lose your 'wood' that way.

You gotta be comfortable to give a strong performance. If you're not, change your position or tell the director. A good director will make sure it's comfortable for you so you can do your best. But I've done scenes out in the middle of the desert, with winds blowing, heat, on a rock with no comforts to speak of, and an anal scene to boot! But for some reason, the scene turned out to be awesome, because the girl I was working with—Alexandra Silk, she hosts 'Sex Court' on the Playboy Channel—she was so supportive and so with me that we just killed. Despite the conditions being the worst.

Greg Dark is a director who puts you in totally uncomfortable situations and then just sits back to see how it all plays out. He'll put a pig mask on you; you won't usually be in a bedroom but in some bizarre location—sometimes great things happen, sometimes they don't.

ANA: *What is the worst experience you've ever had on a shoot?*

GUY: Working for John Leslie, one of the legends of this business. I actually rent his stuff, it's so good. He called me up once to work for him, and I was very excited. I showed up for the shoot and I just was not happening that day. It killed me for two weeks afterwards: 'I fucked up for the Master!' See the thing is: I had John in my head: 'Oh, I'm working for John Leslie.' For some reason that didn't happen with John Stagliano because he's very informal and easygoing. But John Leslie is a very intense man. I hung in there, but I didn't even have sex because I wasn't hard enough. I worked around it because another guy was taking care of the girl and I just stayed at the edge of the scene, talking and playing with myself. I kinda made it work and I did cum, but it just didn't happen. It wasn't Leslie or the girl, it was me. I didn't blame anyone. Any time you have problems the worst thing to do is assign blame to anyone or anything. Just shut up and take it. Don't say "Oh, the girl isn't attractive' or 'I didn't sleep good last night' or "I didn't eat.' That doesn't wash. When you fuck up, just take it, because making excuses just makes you look worse. I apologized to John Leslie, but even he said, 'Well, you fucked up; but I've done it, too.'

Another bad one was something called *Anal Contest* for Tight Ends Productions. Ron Jeremy was the host, and he was onstage in the studio, and there was a whole audience of street people that they invited to watch. So imagine about 50 people, a lot of them homeless, literally roaring you on: 'Come on! Do her in the ass!' and things like that. I had the unlucky task of being the first guy that came out. So Ron Jeremy says, 'Okay, our first contestants are Nicole London and Guy DeSilva!' And all these people are clapping and you walk out naked and are supposed you get it up, do an anal, and cum in less than 20 minutes. They actually time you with a stopwatch! I was definitely trying to block everything out, pretend that the people weren't there. I got it up, I did the anal, but I didn't cum. And Dave Hardman came out and couldn't get it up *at all!* But he improvised. He came out with a girl named Miora, who is one of the 'nastiest' girls in the business. She will do just about anything.

ANA: *Is there anything you won't do on-camera?*

GUY: Yeah, spitting on girls. I'm not into that. For some reason, I'd rather see a woman spit on a guy than a guy on a girl. I don't know why. I'm not into degrading, smacking around or choking girls. I've had some girls ask me to do certain things to them. Some girls like to be smacked around a little. Like I don't mind pulling their hair but not to the point where it hurts. Some girls really want some crazy, extreme stuff, and that's really not my style. Some girls like to be 'pounded' and I don't mind doing that. It's the degrading stuff I don't like.

ANA: *I assume you do only straight porn and don't cross over into gay, right?*

GUY: *[Laughs]* That's the first thing I should've made clear: I don't do gay. Most actresses won't work with guys who do gay stuff, even though the gay stuff is safer and takes more health precautions than we do because of AIDS. They always use condoms.

ANA: *I've read that there are a few white actresses who refuse to work with black actors. Is this true?*

GUY: Yeah, that's a good subject you brought up. A lot of girls, especially girls from the South, and a lotta girls who dance around the country say that in the South if you work with black guys, your rate is not going to be as high. This is just talk, mind you. You have girls who come into the business who say they won't do black guys and they won't do anals—a month later you see them dong an anal scene with Sean Michaels because he's a big name. I've worked with at least 15 to 20 girls who said they didn't do interracial—but for me, I'm of mixed race. In this business, that makes me sort of a chameleon. They use me for a lot of different ethnic roles, which actually works in my favor. There have been girls who have said, 'I won't work with black guys, but I'll work with Guy DeSilva.' I don't know how to take that. Sometimes, with my peers, other black actors have said, 'Why does he get all the work and not me? I'm black, too.' I get that a lot. Sometimes a girl doesn't even realize that I'm black, and then they'll find out later and then they realize it didn't make any difference. So in that way I hope that I'm breakin' down some doors. I look at it that way.

There's been a thing going around the business lately that the black guys don't get it up as good as the white guys, which is not necessarily true. A lot of the black actors, and there are only a handful, don't get the chance to work on the kind of productions that the white guys do. The budgets are also a lot lower for black productions. But that's changing. Sean [Michaels] is one of the most influential black male performers in the business. He wanted to stop just making 'black films' and just make movies for everybody. Mr. Marcus has done pretty well for himself. This guy Byron Long gets work a lot. A new guy, Lexington Steele, he's doing pretty well. There's Santino Lee, who I know well. There's a good solid group of black male performers.

ANA: *What about the black women in the business? How are they treated?*

GUY: Not as good as the rest. Video Team is a company that does quality black product. They spend time on their boxes, they pay good, the production values mean a lot. But you have a lot of lower-budget companies just churning out this inferior black product. It makes the rest of us look bad.

I don't get typecast into 'black' roles like 'The Pimp' or 'The Drug Dealer.' I played a robber once; never again! It just wasn't me. I get a lot of nice guy, gentlemanly roles. And gangsters. One writer told me I look like a 40s movie-star who played gangsters. People tell me a lot that I look like someone from another era. So anytime they're looking for roles like that, I get a lot of calls. Believe it or not, I've actually been sent home from black shoots because they tell me, 'Guy, you're just not black enough!'

ANA: *Do you like reading stuff about yourself in the adult press?*

GUY: Yeah, I'll occasionally check out what people are saying about me. I know a lot of the reviewers, and if it's not good, they just won't say anything about me at all. They won't even mention me. I prefer that, rather than being dogged. Occasionally, they'll say stuff like 'the girl totally dominated the scene—but Guy looked liked he was about ready to pass out.' *[Laughs]* And that's fine with me. If a girl is aggressive and wants to dominate, I won't fight her, I'll let her go. I can be submissive or dominant in a scene. I don't always have to be Macho Man. Sometimes it turns out good when you turn the tables.

ANA: *Have you benefitted from being in porn in any noticeable financial way? I mean, do you look around your apartment or house and think, 'Yeah, this is the life; this is worth it'?*

GUY: To tell you the truth, I think I should be doing a lot better than I am. Every time I make a gang of money it just goes in no time. It just doesn't last. It's not like I have a bunch of money saved up or anything. I need to do more, like direct or produce, than just be talent. You can't really make a whole lot of money just performing, unless you're really good at squaring away money to save.

ANA: *Do you have any other side pursuit besides the adult business?*

GUY: Nope. The adult business is all I do: movies, magazine and print stuff, Internet stuff. But I'd really like to get behind the camera. I've been watching it long enough; believe me, I definitely could do it. I've talked to a lot of fans in the business and kind of put together what they like and what I like seeing. I like to see a lot of tease. I don't like when they cut to the bedroom and the people are already going at it. I like to lead up to the sex, like John Stagliano. Promise it but just tease you along enough.

ANA: *Has the business changed for the actors in the last five to six years?*

GUY: It has, mainly because of the recent AIDS scare. Now, there's a lot more condom use and people are a lot more selective about what they will do. I have never personally known or met anybody in this business who has contracted AIDS. You would think the business would be running rampant with it, but we're a close knit group of people and we get tested every month. That's still not 100%, but it's a good way to at least make some effort to avoid it. Condoms just double the safety.

ANA: *Are there different kinds of preferred lube for anal and vaginal sex?*

GUY: Yes. Astroglide is the best for vaginal but not for anal because it stings the girls. Simple K-Y Jelly is the best for anal.

ANA: *What would make you leave the business for good?*

GUY: Ah, if I couldn't get it up anymore. That and being treated badly, which I won't put up with anyway. If the rates went down, I'd probably leave. Or if the AIDS thing started to getting really bad, the health issue would do it too.

ANA: *What's the worst part of being an adult film actor?*

GUY: If you're doing an anal, and the girl didn't do a proper enema, and she's on top of you and she gets off... you figure out the rest.

ANA: *Yikes...*

GUY: Yeah, I've seen it happen. The best thing to do is just put it right out of your mind. Just wash up down there and don't even look down while you're doing it.

ANA: *How does one know if one is emotionally and physically ready to enter life as a porn actor?*

GUY: If they're fuckin' horny as hell. If you can be so horny to the point that you don't care if anyone's watching you, you can do this. If you can do it for the 'sport' of it, great. But if you're doing it trying to look for a girlfriend or something, it's the wrong business. It's literally 'sport fucking' is what it is.

ANA: *What's the best part about being an adult film actor?*

GUY: Being able to just wake up in the morning and meet a brand new beautiful girl you've never seen before in your life and before you know it, you're having sex with her. In minutes. I find that part fascinating.

ANA: *Doesn't that make it seem all the more lonely, empty or superficial?*

GUY: No, it's kind of a turn-on. Because you don't know what's going to happen. You have no clue.

D. THE LEADING LADIES

The adult sex industry is built almost entirely on its female talent. Jim South of World Modeling Agency estimates that there are 500 to 600 women working today, with another 20 new arrivals walking through his door on a weekly basis. Jim claims he needs to keep around 150 people working a week just to break even.

"Basically for a woman to enter this business is very, very easy," sex star Annabel Chong told me at the VSDA convention. "However, it's also very competitive and this, after all, is California. L.A. is like a beach fitness town; these girls who get off the bus from Nebraska are up against a lot of competition." Almost everyone in porn agrees that while women are somewhat pampered by the X industry, their careers tend to be more short-lived than the men's, partially because of the sheer numbers of girls who want to break in.

From gang bangs to documentaries, Annabel Chong has done it all.

It's true there is a lot of competition among female performers in X, yet strangely there is rarely a shortage of supply or demand. "I can find work for almost any [woman]," Jim South told *Los Angeles* magazine. "Little people, heavyset girls, girls over six feet, girls with small breasts, girls with enormous breasts, black girls, Asian girls, girls of mixed race, Hispanic women, European women, older women..." A female can literally show up at an agent's office on Monday, be working Tuesday through Friday, and then never work again if she doesn't want to. It's that simple. As a porno starlet, you could probably do three scenes a day if you chose to. Jim claims that if you are a female between the ages of 18 to 28 and you are relatively attractive and in good physical shape, you can be working that afternoon if you want to.

For some people, it is only a matter of making some quick cash and getting out. There are others who aim to be "stars" but they haven't thought of exactly how they are going to achieve that stardom. The adult industry draws all types of females, from 19-year-old virgins to professional strippers to women in their 30s who can't get enough sex and figure they might as well get paid for it. You'd be surprised how many female performers are mothers who take care of their children and go to Church on Sunday! Remember, being a porn starlet means slipping into a persona, a role, an identity—you can be whoever you want to be. Lovette called it "flipping into the Lovette mode." Savannah collected all of the things written about her in the press and crossed out every mention of her real name—Shannon Wilsey. Most of the females I've talked to figure it's better than working at McDonald's or at a telemarketing company, so what the hell?

There are also women who are terrified that people will find out. To be quite honest, if you are part of the latter group you shouldn't even be in this business. Even if you think you know what you are getting into, think and think and think again. Especially, you should think about the impact of your decision on friends and family. Often, the problem for female performers is not getting in but getting out of the adult sex industry. Many of the new generation of porn starlets are exotic dancers who enter the business for short periods of time, just long enough to make a few films, appear on a few box covers and then quadruple their salaries as 'featured dancers' who can make as much as $16,000-$20,000 per week doing 20 minute routines on the strip circuit.

The huge growth in the hardcore video business during the 1980s coincided with the opening of large strip clubs all over the country. Rob Abner, who publishes *Stripper* magazine, estimates that the number of strip clubs doubled between 1987 and 1992. Today there are about 2,500 of these clubs nationwide. The salaries of featured dancers, different from 'house' dancers because the clubs pay *them* to dance, have risen astronomically. Besides the top featured dancers, top porn actresses can earn between $8,000 and $15,000 a week. Featured dancers are paid, for the most part, according to the 'credits' they have accumulated—their appearances in hardcore films, on video-box covers, and in men's magazines. "In the hierarchy of sex workers, strippers always used to look down on porn stars, viewing their work with distaste," reported *U.S. News & World Report*. "Now strippers from all over the U.S. (and beyond) are flocking to SoCal and competing for roles in hardcore films."

Then there are the young females who get into the industry, do a bunch of movies, make a bunch of money and then get stuck and can't find any more work. That's the difference between the actresses who get in for months and those who stay in for years. It can play serious games with your head. You may think you are going to be a star, only to discover you are just the flavor of the month. This is why porn has such a high turnover rate amongst its women: every week, 7 to 10 girls leave the Industry and 15 to 25 girls come in. Male performers seem to have an easier time coping with the 'sex object factor,' probably because society doesn't stigmatize them as much as women for being openly sexual.

Yet this hasn't stopped the tide. If anything, the influx of beautiful women has only increased. "I can't explain why beautiful women are still flocking to the business, even more so than in the old days," marveled Jerry Butler. Newcummers are often working at extremely low rates—some will do an anal scene for $300—and often do free boxcovers, hence making it harder for starlets who've been in the business longer.

Fortunately, there are many new markets for porn to absorb the increase in female performers. Nina Hartley, ever the tireless campaigner for women in the business, admitted to me that porn is no different from "98% of all business in the U.S. in that it's still dominated by men, the good and bad ones." Yet according to annual retailers' surveys in *Adult Video News*, women account for 25% of adult sales and rentals in America. This expanding market for female consumers of porn is being targeted by a few smart cookies like Jill Kelly, Nina Hartley, Kym Wilde, Janine Lindemulder, Rebecca Bardoux, Juli Ashton and Ona Zee—women who are directing and producing their own films and heading up their own small sex empires. Big women directors include Toni English, Brandy Alexandre, Tianna Collins and Candida Royale. There are even 90s feminists who support pornography and women's right to both buy it and star in it—women like Camille Paglia, Lisa Palac, Susie Bright, Erica Jong, Laura Kipnis, Sallie Tisdale and Tammy Cole.

The proof, however, is in the testimonies of the female performers who insist that they love what they do. Kitty Monroe told Harris Gaffin that she "was once a skinny, unpopular high school girl" but that after making it in the sex business she had "a lot more self-esteem...It's given me a lot of insight into myself and who I can be. I can be pretty-in-pink or a slut!" Jordan St. James, the hottest newcomer of 1994, told *Marie Claire* magazine that being a celebrity and the self-confidence that came with it was a stark contrast to her childhood: "I left home at 13 and became a ward of the state. My parents were drug addicts. I had a rough time but now things are great. I travel, I meet great people—my life is pretty luxurious!"

Money. In porn's Golden Age, actresses like Seka and Marilyn Chambers earned between $10,000 to $20,000 per movie. Nowadays, the highest paid performers are actresses with exclusive contracts at companies like Vivid and Wicked. A "Vivid girl" earns between $80,000 and $100,000 a year for appearing in about 20 sex scenes (usually five to eight films per year) and making around a dozen personal appearances. Only around ten to fifteen women in the industry are signed to such contracts. Top starlets who are not signed to contracts and act as freelance performers can make as much as $5,000 to $7,000 a day. Other starlets are paid roughly $1,000 to $1,500 per sex scene. A typical pay scale might read something like this: fellatio, $300-$350; lesbian scene, $400-$600; boy-girl scene, $500-$700; double penetration, $800-$2,000; anal, double anal, double vaginal: $1,000 and up. No tax or social security is deducted from a porn star's pay, but performers have to pay taxes on their earnings just like any "normal" American. In one year, a woman who really shakes her tail can appear in up to 100 films. "If she is noticed by one of the larger studios, she next lands a contract," writes *Los Angeles* magazine. "[She] works only in said studio's films, draws as much as $100,000 a year and then launches herself onto the international dance circuit, earning up to $20,000 a week stripping three times a day and selling autographed pictures and other associated items of her being."

Actresses are paid on a day rate for a 12-hour shoot day, in which usually 2 to 3 scenes can be shot. As in Hollywood, the demand is greatest for actresses in their 20s. Sometimes an actress's age determines her fee— 27 is the average age when the money starts to plummet. Many starlets supplement their on-camera careers with exotic dancing, fan clubs, mail-order businesses, private parties and Internet sites. We will discuss these options in the 'Branching Out' section.

Women in the X industry, especially the newer generation, are notorious for their money problems. Take Tori Welles, the first superstar of the early 90s: when she was 13 she reportedly gave a blowjob to a guy in exchange for a ride to Hollywood. After she became famous in porn, she had a beautiful house in Topanga Canyon, a nanny for her two children, a "nice Jewish husband" and a $15,000 a week gig dancing at strip clubs nationwide. By 1999, she was hustling as a production assistant on porn shoots to support her two kids.

Your Fans. Bill Margold started an organization called Friends of X-rated Entertainment (F.O.X.E.), which attempts to connect "respectable" porn fans to porn stars over a course of conventions and awards ceremonies each year. It's sort of like a big group fan-club. One of the reasons Margold started the club is because of his belief that "the people who make porn today have an abysmal disrespect for the people who consume it." The common perception among industry insiders is that porn fans are derelict losers with low intelligence. Not only is this completely wrong—many porn consumers earn six figure incomes and have prestigious positions in society—but it is a sure-fire way to shortchange your career. Like my friend Mariah, you may have worked phone sex or done lap-dancing before you got into porn; you may have seen the worst side of men and their peculiar sexual tastes. But, simply put, if it wasn't for them you wouldn't be working right now. The fans are the source of the attention so many actors and actresses crave.

Besides, most porn stars supplement their film, dancing and modeling income by having fan clubs. Sometimes the fan clubs are run by their studio. Joy King, the publicity director of Wicked Pictures, runs Jenna Jameson's fan club—but this is extremely rare. Most of the time, the starlet's boyfriend, mom, roommate, high-school buddy or else the starlet herself runs her own fan club and responds to the often huge amounts of mail she gets. A rundown of the perks for joining contract-girl Stacy Valentine's fan club is a good example of the typical membership package offered:

> *2 personally autographed 8 x 10 color photographs*
> *Letter welcoming you to the club*
> *Biography*
> *Newsletter*
> *Filmography: a current list of her movies*
> *Membership card*
> *Catalog*
> *Valentine's Day card*

Many porn stars have found that the best way to advertise their fan clubs is by simply putting the fan club contact info at the end of the credits of their films. Numerous porn stars, including Christi Lake, Kim Chambers, Brittany O'Connell, Misti Hills, Alyssa Haven, Tyffany Minx, Melanie Stone and Dave Cummings also have their own websites.

There are times, like in the careers of David Letterman, Tom Cruise, Brad Pitt or Shania Twain, when some fans may go overboard in their fascination with a celebrity figure. Porn especially draws male fans who aren't "quite right in the head." Female porn stars like Savannah, Asia Carrera, and Sharon Mitchell have been stalked by such types. Lovette, in particular, had an unusually frightening experience with a customer she gave private dances to: he pulled a knife on her during one of their sessions. After she called the police, they came and arrested the man, who as it turned out had a folder of Lovette's magazine layouts and newspaper clippings of her club schedules. Lying on top of the folder was a loaded

Uzi submachine gun.

On March 30, 1996, Sharon Mitchell finished a show at a strip club and was approached by a guy who wanted to have sex for money. Sharon was not into it. He tried to rape her, biting her savagely all over her body and crushing her larynx. She passed out and almost died, but in a fit of self-preservation she woke up and knocked out her would-be rapist with one of her exercise weights. Sharon's always been a bit of an exercise freak. "We later found out he had killed two other women," Sharon told Reuters. "I turned my life around at that point... and [Bill Margold's] Protecting Adult Welfare was there for me."

This is why porn shoots have security guards. This is why many porn shoots are closed to the public. This is why, at Bill Margold's F.O.X.E. Awards, porn fans who paw, mistreat or disrespect the stars are either slapped or escorted out by the security detail. It also helps to have a big ex-Marine boyfriend who can stand behind you with his arms folded menacingly (whether you are a man or a woman).

Attitude. Newcummers to the adult industry often think that they need to toot their own horn and claw their way to the top, much like in the predatory corporate world. In fact, some of the most successful porn stars are surprisingly humble and low-key. For instance, Stephanie Swift has built a huge following without copping any attitude at all. "I'm not a competitive-type person," she confided to me. "I just enjoy this and I'm comfortable with who I am. I don't have many insecurities about myself or what I'm doing."

Bill Margold says that the best porn actresses are at heart, "naughty little girls who seem innocent and pure on the outside but, on the inside, they just love to lift their skirts for all the boys in the neighborhood." At a recent lecture, Nina Hartley described herself as someone who would "have sex on a stage in front of rows of bleachers and charge festival setting." And Nina is known in the Industry as the consummate professional.

The makers of porn films have a strange conflict: they thrive on the newest girl, the latest flavor of the month, yet the new girls are often the most annoying to work with. The average porn filmmaker is willing to tolerate first-day jitters, but only to a point. The director needs his female talent to do what the script requires and do it well, regardless of her personal feelings. She may be in pictures she doesn't like, or she may have things she won't do or people she won't do it with, but any new girl should remember the following: they hired you, you agreed to the terms, so go in there and do what you supposed to do—it's your job. Don't be a prima donna or a diva. Your payback is in the films you will get hired to do and the exposure you will get from them. Then, if you are thinking of going long-term, you can start to build yourself a reputation.

Your Career. Teri Weigel is one of the few females to cross over in reverse: she started as a hallowed *Playboy* playmate, probably the only adult-industry honor more glamorous than being a Vivid contract girl. (Her reason: "I love to suck dick!")

In the porn world, the top of the career mountain is the contract girl—and the top of that is the pampered, glamorous "Vivid Queen." Wicked, VCA, Ultimate, Metro and Sin also sign exclusive contracts, but with only a maximum of three female performers at any given time. Vivid leads the pact with 15 contract girls. The first Vivid girl was Ginger Lynn Allen. Started in 1984 with just two employees, Vivid is now a $20-million a year company with 100 employees, producing 8-16 movies a month with state-of-the-art digital equipment on their own premises. Vivid players make a lot of money working on fewer films than any other actresses in the business. The length of a contract can vary. One year renewable is the average. Given the chance, almost everybody renews. The contract gives the performers a large say in whom they work with, as far as additional actresses are concerned, as well as directors. Though they don't get script approval, they do get input. If they are interested and show some directing talent, contract players are often encouraged to make their own films. Vivid queens may also serve as corporate sponsors, attend stock car rallies, open football and baseball games, appear in art galleries, and much more. Vivid even hosted a "Club Porno."

Contract girls have a lot of power, too. Many observers of the X-rated industry have noticed that Wicked films was just a wannabe studio, a pretender to the throne of Steve Hirsch's Vivid. One girl—Jenna Jameson—completely turned the Wicked studio when she became a superstar of unprecedented proportions. Now Jenna is arguably the most famous porn starlet on the planet.

So how do you get to be a contract girl? Let's be honest: you can plan a short-term or long-term career, but the bottom line is that fame is not something you can easily control. When I asked VCA contract-girl Stacy Valentine how she managed to climb so high in the industry, she admitted to being mystified herself. "I don't do hardly anything anymore and my name has gotten bigger," she explained. "It's time, I think. I've been in the business three years and it took me two years before my name was recognizable."

Obviously, not everyone achieves their ultimate goals. "The vast majority of porn actresses are 'B girls' who earn about $300 a scene," *U.S. News* reported in 1997. "They typically try to do two scenes a day, four or five times a week." Perhaps rather than aiming for the top, you too should shoot for being a second tier performer. A modest ambition can lead to more jobs without the sometimes intense pressure of being a superstarlet or a contract girl.

Besides, even if you can avoid the stress and pressure, there is still the risk of overexposure—another peril for the porn star who works too much rather than not enough. Nina Hartley, in particular cautions against this; she experienced an almost devastating career slump in 1987. The only way she got through it was through her sheer will power. Nina told me how she did it:

NINA HARTLEY: *I wasn't always on top. I managed to end up on top by sheer stubbornness and a refusal to leave. In years 4-6, there was definitely a slump in the Industry and if I didn't have dancing to fall back on I would have wondered what the hell was going on. If I hadn't been so stubborn and so into the business I would've gone: 'They don't love me anymore; I'm leaving!' I just wouldn't leave! I'm in Adult for a reason and that's to be a teacher. I had to hang in long enough to become a 'classic'—it took ten years. I have a lot of fans, people who know me, fans who love me. My fans have always been very loyal to me and very, very supportive. Now, all the writing I've done over the years, all the interviews I've given, the TV I've done—just to preach the message of 'Sex Positivism.' It's sheer perseverance.*

Nina Hartley prepares to give an unforgettable lecture.

Currently, Nina spends about half of her year—around two weeks out of every month—on the road, dancing in clubs four to six nights a week. Dancing is the bulk of her income, not her movies. She has appeared in over 300 hardcore films since the early 1980s, not that much considering Peter North has appeared in 1,400. Nina also puts out her own line of sex-therapy tapes with titles like *Nina Hartley's Guide to Foreplay, Nina Hartley's Guide to Private Dancing, Nina Hartley's Guide to Better Fellatio* and *Nina Hartley's Guide to Anal Sex.* (They are available through the North Carolina mail-order company Adam & Eve.) She writes magazine articles and books, and she teaches and lectures at speaking engagements across the country.

Boxcovers. Companies like Vivid and Wicked elevated the look of porn box covers from sleazy shots of cum-drenched faces and goo-glazed body parts to high-class designs that look more like Victoria's Secret ads than pornography. These days, shooting box covers is almost a separate industry in itself, and girls have found that box covers not only get them extra money but also extra exposure (and therefore better treatment) when they go on the dance circuit. Box covers can be an ego or self-esteem thing for certain girls—who wouldn't want to be paid to be shown in glorious, airbrushed perfection looking like a million bucks? (There are exceptions, like the genres called 'Amateur' or 'Gonzo' porn, which shoot their boxcovers right on top of the sex being filmed.)

No question about it, the box cover is one of the most important marketing tools when it comes to selling porn. Of course, some companies go for shock value, so you may not always agree with or like the names they slap on the films you made, like *Cuckoo For Cocoa Cock, Gangbang Face Bath, Cum-Buttered Cornholes, Jizz-Glazed Goo Guzzlers* or *Ass-Worshipping Rim Jobbers.* C'est la vie. That's ze way of ze porn world.

Don't Get Scammed. Porn Stars, like the stars in "regular" show biz, have to be prepared to swim with the sharks. Occasionally, those sharks will have all the money and all the power and will want you to demonstrate your desire to be a porn star in a very physical fashion—on them. Other times, they will fail to live up to their promises or they will spread false rumors. Every male and female performer has such stories. Annabel Chong banged 70 men 251 times and was never paid for it. It all goes back to what female director Candida Royale said: "You'd better go in knowing at all times what you want to get out of it and what you're prepared to give." This means knowing what you will and will not do. This means not showing up to a set and being talked into an anal when you've specified "no anal!"

No employer who is reputable will make you do something you don't want to do, but again the strength to say no or to stand your ground and negotiate what you think you deserve must lie within you. The difference is between having inhibitions and having limitations. Even if you have no inhibitions, it only makes sense that you would have some limitations. No sensible performer would be willing to do absolutely anything, and producers will respect you for sticking to your guns.

The actress Ona Zee was grossly underpaid by the industry—she made only $450 a day, less than most men—mainly because she was considered "older." Rather than slink away and disappear, she tried to unionize workers in the porn industry. She failed, mainly due to the fast turnover of workers and the legally outcast nature of the business. However, it started women talking about organizing and finding a voice. As we will see in the 'Branching Out' section, women like Ona got their revenge.

Today, there is no real watchdog organization for the Industry to help performers steer clear of disreputable employers. The closest is a section on journalist Luke Ford's website (www.lukeford.com) called "Ethics Rankings," which star-rates each producer, director and company according to their "trustability." The rankings can be very helpful if you want to get some background on a company or person you are considering doing business with.

What To Bring To The Set. Like your leading lord, you should come prepared to play a variety of roles, which means bringing at least one change of clothes, lingerie, underwear, etc. Unless you are doing a specialty video featuring women with hairy legs, pits, or beards, you should shave and keep yourself well-groomed. This means showering and washing your pubic area with a little soap and cup of hot water. Bring along your own germicidal soap, deodorant, mouthwash and a soft toothbrush. Do not floss or use a hard toothbrush before a sex scene: blood from little cuts in your gums does not look good smeared on a guy's cock. Also remember to bring your own water. And don't forget your script if they sent it to you—it shows you are a true professional!

Besides your choice of birth control, douching is the most important way to keep good-smelling and kissable clean. Again, your own preference for douches comes into play here, but I suggest you stay away from the "fancier" brands of scented douche; they only contain perfumes and dyes, and you shouldn't be putting any unnatural chemicals inside you. (For more info on what you should bring to the set, see Chapter 1's Porn Profile and the advice Bill Margold gives to the young starlet, Mariah Wind.)

Blowjobs. A porn movie without a good shaft-licking is like a lemonade stand without ice cubes. Be prepared to demonstrate this skill, and practice if you haven't. If you're unsure of what technique to adapt, just watch some good blowjobbers in action: Tori Welles, Anna Malle, Marilyn Chambers, Jill Kelly, Madison, Candy Apples, Ashlyn Gere and, of course,

Linda ("Deep Throat") Lovelace and Little Oral Annie. Bunny Bleu once sucked cock while humming 'Old MacDonald'—probably a concentration method.

On Luke Ford's website, director Patrick Collins summed up his eight requirements for an all-time great blowjob:

> *Cock adoration bordering on worship*
> *Asking, begging, pleading for cum*
> *Asking for [the actor] to cum on her face*
> *Lots of spit and drool and slurping*
> *Acknowledging that she knows he loves it*
> *Ball licking and sucking*
> *The blowjob lasts a long time*
> *More than sucking: light teeth raking, slapping dick on face, etc.*

Facials. Facials are common in porn, as most male viewers like to see cum on a woman's face. Many women don't like facials but put up with them. Women usually don't get extra money for doing a facial, but the smart ones know a director or a company's particular style before they go on the set. For example, if you agree to work for a company that specializes in videos showing guys cumming all over women's faces, you know what they're going to want from you. If you are talking to someone who is filming a porn video independently, ask for their requirements on facials, especially since AIDS can be transmitted from semen getting in your eyes. Keep in mind, if you are on the fence about facials, that cum is protein-rich and good for the skin and hair.

Anals. Anal is a relatively new thing in porn films. It didn't become hugely popular among filmmakers and consumers alike until the mid-80s, when Bruce Seven released *Aerobisex Girls*. Erica Boyer and Keli Richards were among the first stars of backdoor cinema. Now, innovators like Rex Borksy and the notorious Max Hardcore bang out anal-themed films for a nearly flooded market. Some current anal queens include Brittany Stryker, Nici Sterling, J.R. Carrington, Nikki Sinn, Roxanne Hall, Lovette, Rachel Ryan and Sheri St. Claire. Many actresses say "no anal" but end up doing it for various personal or professional reasons—like Asia Carerra or Savannah. As a newcummer, you shouldn't feel you have to go directly to anal, unless it's something you're really into. In my opinion, you should never do anal for any less than $1,000. Director Ed Powers is rumored to pay up to $10,000 for a woman's first on-screen experience with anal sex. But if your partner uses no condom, that could expose you to an STD like AIDS—and, honey, the money ain't worth dying for.

Luckily many of the bigger companies require condoms on set. If not, producers require that every performer get an AIDS test at least every three months, if not every month, and you are required to bring a photocopy of the negative test results to every shoot you go to. Female performers should also clean themselves with an enema before doing anal. (Fleet is a popular brand of enemas among porn females.) Not doing so can result in a messy, embarrassing scene for you, your male costar and the 20 or so people standing around watching.

Often, women aren't properly introduced to anal sex. You do need to do some preparation to enjoy it. Your muscles should be relaxed and receptive, and your partner should begin the penetration with slow, gradual movements. Christie Lake recommends "lotsa lube"—Astroglide and Wet are popular brands. For orgies or gang-bangs olive oil is actually preferred to baby oil. In the short term, if you consider doing on-camera anal, you had better eat light beforehand. Salads are preferred foods to eat before receiving anal sex, as they are light foods that serve to help clean out your system. In the long term, you should remember two things: (1) doing a lot of anal could lead to intestinal and rectal problems when you get older; and (2) anal increases your risk of getting the HIV virus and possibly developing full-blown AIDS. So if an actor or a director's promises don't seem right to you, you have every right to raise your concerns. Demand to see the HIV results of your costars if you feel you need to. They have to bring them to the shoot anyway, so don't worry if they get a little snippy. It's your life!

Girl-Girl, Gay & Bi. "Girl-girl" has always been a thriving subgenre in porno. Lesbian action is preferred by filmmakers and editors because it's easier to cut for the cable softcore markets, and many female performers prefer being with other women than men. Janine Lindemulder, Vivid's top contract girl, had a very business-savvy clause written into her contract: she will not have sex with men on-camera, only women. As a result of this clever move, Janine is now the top porn actress of the 90s because of what she *won't* do. Men rent her movies to see whether, this time, she'll relent and take a cock or two. Janine once bragged to a reporter that, because of her girl-only career, she could "write her own check" should she ever decide to finally do a man on camera.

Also, for women, bisexuality seems to come easier in a society where the female image has been so sexualized. Many women in porn have this bisexual quality; in fact, it is hard to think of one who doesn't. However, if a male actor knows your work and sees you enjoying 'girl-girl' more than 'girl-boy' it might dampen his drive and affect his performance, and then you'll be cooling your heels. Also, if you do bisexual films—in which men make love to you as well as each other—there might be a stigma hanging over you. Actress Jeanna Fine made quite a few movies for Catalina Video, a company that specializes in gay and bisexual porn, and men like Jerry Butler were reluctant to work with her. Of course, Fine also used intravenous drugs like heroin, so this contributed even more to the wariness of her male co-stars.

Your Performance. It isn't necessary, but it certainly helps if you are enthusiastic in front of the camera. Sometimes even the top stars don't have to do much beyond showing up. Jenna Jameson's performances can vary, but some critics are of the opinion that she doesn't fake it well enough; Savannah's sex scenes were almost universally panned as being 'wooden,' 'dead,' 'boring' or 'phoned in.' Yet these women made up to $200,000 a year as porn's top sex queens.

On the other hand, especially if you are not a Jenna or a Savannah, performing means exactly that: "performing." Some females, like Tigr or Viper, compensated for their modest physical endowments by giving more of themselves during a scene. (Viper was so aggressive she actually took down the indestructible T.T. Boy; "It was almost as if she was starved for sex," Sharon Mitchell, who watched the scene being filmed, told a magazine. "I remember [T.T. Boy] looking at me like, 'Help me!'") There are many other female stars who are good at 'faking it'—or putting on a good show even though they are not into the sex or the man: pros like Nina Hartley and Christy Canyon come to mind. Often the chemistry between an actress and her director can push through a good, if not great, sex performance.

It can also help to approach your leading lord before you shoot your scene and simply ask him what he likes: Biting the nipples? Sucking the fingers? Pulling the hair? Purring? Dirty talk? Another performance edge comes if the porn woman has a dancing history, whether it be classical, exotic, or aerobic. Tasha Voux and Sharon Mitchell were exotic dancers who were also trained as contortionists. Voux could do a handstand or a full split during a sex scene. Viper spent a season with the prestigious American Ballet Theater in New York City and was also a strip-club dancer in Baltimore before she moved to L.A.

Some porn stars have special talents: "squirting" in particular has made for some memorable careers. Nikki Charm was known for giving one of the first visible female 'spurting' orgasms (check out her tape *Talk Dirty to Me One More Time IV*), and legendary actress Veronica Hart supposedly did one before she retired from acting to direct her own films.

Your Body. Equivalent to a man's cock as far as marketability and hireability, your body is the tool of your trade and should be kept in prime condition, like a Formula 5 racing car. Stacy Valentine told me she had four simple secrets for staying in great shape: "Slimfast, special diets, a trainer, and my stairmaster." Each woman's body is special and offers unique pleasures—very much like the fact that no two fingerprints are alike—so your exercise and diet regimen will be different from the next woman's. But you do need to exercise to keep in shape, whether it be Tae Bo or jazz dancing or plain old club dancing. A healthy diet is also advisable. I suggest you stay away from booze, especially if you are working a lot. Some actresses take a drink to relax them before a shoot, and that's fine. If you abuse alcohol, however, your sweat will sting and your body will give off a bad odor.

Many porn stars, like professional athletes, have succeeded in becoming known despite debilitating problems. Because of a childhood accident, Veronica Hart has terrible burns over 25 percent of her body. Her directors shot all her films from a careful angle. In fact, Veronica was rarely fully naked on film—she always had a piece of lingerie draped over her arms or legs. Despite this, she is considered one of the best actresses ever in the history of adult films. Cesarean scars from childbirth can also be hidden with makeup or clothing or tricky camera angles, but they are a bit of a visual hindrance.

Like male porn performers, females often turn their careers on a specific bodily attribute, like Julie Rage, who supposedly has the longest tongue in hardcore. And out of great asses, great porn careers grow: Nina Hartley, Missy, Lana Sands, Tanya Foxx, Danyel Cheeks, Krysti Lynn, Janine Lindemulder and Jenna Jameson are among some of the finest. As for breast augmentation through surgery, this is a decision that only you should make. Often the suggestion to have breast surgery will come when you are in an agent's office (certainly not Bill Margold's, who detests breast implants.) You may already be a dancer and have had the surgery, or you may be thinking about it. Whatever your situation, it is something that you should only do after careful consideration. Most directors will leave it up to you—with some opinionated prodding, I'm sure. Something to think about: only the big companies like Vivid will pay for a girl's breast implant surgery (although Vivid queen Jenteal refuses to get implants). The rest have to foot the bill themselves.

The typical type of surgery received by porn starlets and many mainstream entertainers is the installation of a user-friendly saline-injection valve allowing the woman to go from an A to an E cup and then back again. Many stars have spoken highly of their breast implants, but there are always drawbacks, primarily with scar tissue building up. Savannah had two breast surgeries that helped to ruin her figure: the first was 435 cc of silicone injected into each breast; then a few years later, she had them done with 600 ccs, bringing her up to a 34DD. After the second surgery, her breasts were so large that they wrinkled funny when she leaned over, rippled when she would lie on her back, and had considerable visible scar tissue. Linda Lovelace, America's first porn star, had silicone poisoning from her implants and had to have one of her breasts removed in the late 80s. Girls with grotesquely augmented breasts like Wendy Whoppers or Kimberly Kupps are often considered freaks born out of the obsession for big breasts rampant in 80s porn.

In fact, breast implants became so popular among the starlets of the 80s that in the 90s the business saw a backlash against them. Whole companies have sprung up in opposition to the surgically enhanced superbabes of porn. Realistic Pictures insists on using real-breasted women in their films. Norm Zadeh's *Perfect 10* features women without a stitch of surgery; and top directors like John Leslie, John Stagliano and Patrick Collins prefer more natural females. Some girls try and pass themselves off as "real," but there are ways of telling:

a) *Scars under or around the areola, near the crease where the breast joins the chest, or under the arm pits;*

b) *Substantial bulging in the inner and upper surfaces of the breast, since natural breasts are more flat on these surfaces;*

c) *Breasts that move unnaturally, like "a block of jello."*

As for other augmentations to your body, Jim South cautions against tongue piercings because they give a person a pronounced lisp. Tattoos that are very obvious also might hurt your chances of getting roles. An extreme example was Viper, who entered porn as an oddity because of her elaborate bodywork: a 3-foot serpent tattoo, with a tongue pointing towards her crotch, pierced nipples, and a pierced clitoris. She made only 70 videos in her five year career. If you must, or already have, a tattoo, I recommend that you pay attention to the starlets who have small or demurely placed ones—like Jenna Jameson, who has a heart on her little behind that says "Heartbreaker," and Jill Kelly, who has a heart on her butt and four small Chinese characters around her body.

E. PORN PROFILE: An Interview with Jill Kelly

At 27, Jill Kelly has joined Janine and Jenna Jameson as one of the Three Reigning Queens of modern porn. Jill is the only one who has built her own sex empire instead of establishing her career as a contract girl. No one has ever owned Jill but Jill. She is a new kind of porn woman.

The 5'7", 115-pound, 36D-24-36 actress claims that she has never called people looking for work. They all call her. She is on practically every producer's speed dial. They don't try to scam her because she is strong, takes no shit, and always gives outstandingly sexy performances. Filmmakers also know if they want Jill Kelly, they are going to have to pay top dollar. Recently, she had four auditions for mainstream movies in one week—an unheard of amount for an actress in the porn world. Jill's appeal, besides her classy, cool but unintimidating presence is that she looks like Janine but does things on camera that Janine never would—her double penetration with Eric Price and Peter North in 1997's Persona is about the hottest sex scene in recent memory.

It hasn't all been easy for her. Her parents didn't find out she was in porn until her husband Cal made all the papers by killing himself on her front lawn. Then she was blamed by many in the business for his death. Jill has been fending off offers to turn her and Cal's story into a feature movie: she wants to do it herself and donate all the profits to Survivors of Suicide.

ANA LORIA: *Now that you head up Jill Entertainment, do you have your talent sign exclusive contracts?*

JILL KELLY: My talent doesn't sign exclusive contracts. We used to do that. I was going to sign Bonita Saint, and I did have Devon Davis signed to an exclusive contract. For me it just didn't work out well because not every girl is as hard a worker as me, so it becomes very frustrating. When I say "Be there at ten", I mean be there at ten and on time. Usually, [contract girls] are signed to do like one film a month or one every other month. But Bonita and Devon aren't exclusive with me. In fact, Bonita came to me when she was 18, wanting to get into the business and I said, "No, no, no, you're way too young!" In fact, if you talk to a lot of people in this business, everybody thinks that anybody coming into this business should be 25 and up because it's the decision of a lifetime, and most of them don't understand that. Besides, the younger ones flake out on bookings and don't know how to manage themselves or the money they make—it's all part of being 20, I guess.

ANA: *Before you became a sex mogul you appeared in over 300 films. But you were never a contract girl?*

JILL: Nope. I never signed a contract. I've been offered them, but to me you can make more money on your own; that's the reason why I won't sign any girls. You also get more exposure. You see, under contract someone can be a Wicked girl or a Vivid girl—but there are so many of them already, it's like 'Which is which?' I'd rather do 100 movies than 10 movies a year because there were over 11,000 movies that were released last year. Why would you limit yourself to ten of them? The mass majority of the public is only going to see you in 10 movies—it's going to be harder for you to go dancing on the road. That why I never signed. I mean, I went through Jim South in the beginning, and I'm still with World Modeling out of loyalty to him. I've been with Jim for like five years now. But everybody knows I have my own number.

ANA: *That's interesting, because many people caution against a star 'overexposing' herself, so to speak…*

JILL: You know what? All these warnings about 'overexposure' are a crock of shit. And you can quote me on that. When I got in this business I was working every single day doing movies. Everybody was telling me, "Nobody is going to want to use you because it's going to be too many movies." If you're good, you have star power, your scenes are good, you're professional, you're on time, and your movies sell, then they are going to want to use you. I still get calls for work all the time. I've cut back and jacked my rates up really high because I don't want to do as much. I'd rather do movies for myself where I make all the money. That's the American way.

I have three websites right now, I have my production company Jill Entertainment—we put out about a movie a month. I dance and do my scenes, and I work for Fox magazine, of which I am the Publisher, and Adult Stars magazine.

ANA: *Wow!*

JILL: Yeah, setting up your own business is a lot of hard work, and a lot of girls come into the Industry and think it's going to happen to them overnight. Well, they have another think coming; it's not handed to any of us. We worked hard. Either you got it or you don't. Yeah, it's easy for girls to become an overnight sensation—they THINK, but it doesn't quite work like that. It takes a lot of hard work and dedication to become a star in this business. I just worked my butt off. I'm a workaholic.

ANA: *What do you think are some of the biggest misconceptions about the business?*

JILL: It's definitely not glamorous. It's nice to be pampered and have the makeup artist doing your hair and be shot really beautifully. But you have to keep yourself in shape; you have to keep yourself looking good. It's long hours and tough positions and photo shoots; you're doing it outside, and it's 110 degrees and the wind is blowing your hair in your face. You're in the middle of the desert, and it's dry and the lube is sticking to the condom and it's rubbing you raw. Then there are times where you love the guy or girl you're working with—which means you have good onscreen chemistry, and it's an awesome sex scene and its wasn't too hot or too cold. It's not always so fun. That's a big misconception that a lot of guys I talk to on the road communicate to me. They say, "Oh, how can I get in the business?" I tell them that directors don't want to take chances with new guys; it's easier to use the same five guys because those five guys are guaranteed woodsters. No one wants a guy with hard-on problems—and they all think they can do it. I say, "Imagine ten people around you waiting for you, and maybe you're close to cumming but you keep having to pull it out because you can't cum." They think they can all do it, and when it comes down to it most of them are all talk. I've seen the big shots get down to it and then not be able to perform. Not everybody can be Peter North. I like to do what I'm doing because I know that I'm going to be only so hot for so long, so that's why I strive to make the best out of it and enjoy it and make all the money and learn everything I can.

ANA: *You're actually moving more into the businesswoman/entrepreneur thing, so it actually extends your career past the usual three or four years that is the norm for the average porn actress.*

JILL: Exactly. Now that I'm moving into the more behind-the-camera and the businesswoman thing, I can even stay in the business longer than if I was just acting. Many of the girls are doing this now. Asia Carrera is a good example: she has a website and an edit bay, so she does all the behind-the-scenes stuff. She's another smart one. We've taken what we know, having done so many movies, and we're using it rather than letting it chew us up. Again, these girls come in and they don't save any money, and they have nothing to show for it. Now I direct and produce my own movies. It's very empowering.

ANA: *What, as a director, do you look for in your talent?*

JILL: Beauty, chemistry, and energy. That's why I like people to pick who they want to work with, and I like to use 'strong wood', which means guys who are strong in a scene. Beautiful girls who are still nasty.

ANA: *You encourage talent to send you their shots directly. Are you becoming an alternative to World Modeling?*

JILL: Oh yeah. But it's a small world, and after I signed someone like Bonita Saint I sent her over to World Modeling to get other work with other people. It's a nice interchange of talent, but I'm in no way looking to become an agent. That's not for me.

ANA: *How long did you dance before you entered films?*

JILL: I've been dancing off and on for ten years total. When I was a 'house' dancer I would watch all the 'featured' dancers, most of whom were porn stars, come in and make all the money, get lines of people and get the beautiful pictures. They had it made, and they didn't have to pay the club to work there. The clubs paid them. I thought, 'Shit I could do that!'

ANA: *What was it like filming your first scene?*

JILL: I was with [my husband] Cal, at the time, so it was kind of a turn-on to do it. We had just gotten married, and I didn't want to be with any-one else besides him. The thing I was nervous about was giving a blow job, because I didn't know what my face was going to look like on-cam-era. I just felt I looked so fuckin' weird with a dick in my mouth! And everybody can see your mouth all stretched out. It just doesn't look pret-ty. But you get over that. Plus, back then I wasn't the master cocksucker that I am now. Now I know that every guy's different—just like every girl—and I know I give great head. I'll even ask a guy before a scene what he likes, and I'll do it exactly to a 'T' how they like it. I like to give great blowjobs because—well, who wouldn't want 'em, ya know?

ANA: *Yeah, I saw that amazing one you gave Jon Dough in* **Janine Extreme Close-Up.** *He lasted about two fucking seconds in your mouth. Kudos, Jill.*

JILL: *[Laughs]* Thank You.

ANA: *I heard there was sort of a stigma attached to the men who try to get into the Industry on a woman's coattails. What's your view on that?*

JILL: Oh, are you kidding? Everybody does that. I'm different in that I am all for couples getting into the business together exclusively. I'm totally for that; I think that there's no problem with it. I know how hard relationships can be. Relationships are hard, period, but in this business they're even harder. And I'm a lover, so I like being in a relationship. I don't like being alone. I like having one person who I am with. And in this business, it still hurts—no matter if it's work or not, it's still sex and everybody knows that it's all very enjoyable at times. Some people like myself are very jealous and possessive of whoever. I admit it full-on.

ANA: *You were once a 'new girl' in the Industry. What do you think of the new generations of girls who are entering porn?*

JILL: There are so many girls who come into this business to be famous, they don't even give a shit about the fuckin' money. They want to be the next Jenna Jameson or the next Janine or the next Jill Kelly and let me tell you, it happens everywhere I go. It's not glamorous. Maybe you're having a bad day, maybe your dog just died and someone comes up to you and says, "Oh, are you so-and-so...?", and you're not in the mood. Believe me, when you start to be recognized everywhere and you don't feel like talking to anybody, it can get to be a burden. But those are your fans and those are the people who make your money. I love my fans to death—they are my favorite part of this business, especially when I'm on the road. It's cool because these people, most of them anyway, really love you and actually, honestly care for you. But there are times when it irritates me. A couple of friends of mine who are young just hang out with me because of who I am. And that hurts sometimes. I'm an Aquarius; I love everybody. A lot of girls who, as they get more known, will see that people will try to use them.

ANA: *How do you stay competitive in this business?*

JILL: If you know anything about Aquarians, it's that we're the least competitive people, unless somebody personally challenges us. I'm so uncatty. I love girls—that's partly why I got into this business. At one point I thought I was gay! That's why it's so funny when I see girls get catty or jealous or competitive. I don't ever want to be like that. I think women are beautiful, and I think if everybody wasn't so insecure about themselves it would make it a bit easier, a bit more fun.

ANA: *Do you watch your own movies?*

JILL: Out of the 300 I've done, I've probably watched about 30 of them. I tend to criticize myself and my performance too much. Everybody does that to themselves when they see themselves on camera. When I'm a director, that's when I think I'm too nice for talent. That's my only downfall, I think.

F. BRANCHING OUT

The Women. Porn is hard to do as just a part-time job if you're a woman, partly because the money is so good and partly because there are so many offshoots a woman can take advantage of. After all, you carry all the "goods" on your person—you *are* "the goods"—so why not try to make as much from it as possible? When not doing films, an average porn starlet can dance, model for box covers, do oil and sex-toy ads, appear in magazines and calendars, sell molds of her private parts, the list goes on and on. Porn stars can also make a fair share of their money running fan clubs with merchandise to sell, from signed pictures to 'used' panties or even 'used' dildos. And then, of course, there are the lucrative personal appearances at adult book stores, selling signed posters and doing nude Polaroids for fans.

In other words, women are turning into sex moguls. Christi Lake started her own company Dripping Wet Pix and virtually invented the concept of the "fan fuck." Ex-wrestler Tiffany Million launched her own string of porn videos, Immaculate Video Conceptions. During 1996 and 1997, Shane, former sidekick of porn producer Seymour Butts, put out her own line of video hardcore, *Shane's World*, which has been a big financial success. Jill Kelly started Jill Kelly Entertainment and created the immensely popular *Perfect Pink* series and now searches for talent like any other producer/director. Even Ona Zee got her revenge on those who underpaid her because she was "too old" by starting the successful Ona Zee Pictures.

Although it's rare, some successful porn careers have been supplemented by prostitution, especially those of gay porn stars. Since I advocate legal and safe-sex, I cannot endorse this line of work. In states where it is permissable, a wiser alternative might be "custom-made" videos, where wealthy customers commission a video to be shot to their exact requirements. If a woman accepts such an order, she can get a trusted party to video her as she performs and talks to the camera/client.

The Men. Despite the fact that male porn actors seem to stay in the business longer than the women, they have rarely branched out by selling and marketing their own images. Instead, many male actors become directors during or after their on-camera careers. Randy West, Chuck Martino, Jake Steed, Jeff Stryker, and Peter North are all directing or have their own "lines" now, including Randy West's *Up and Cummers* and Peter North's *The North Pole.* Even Dave Cummings, a fiftysomething ex-Army colonel, has marketed himself as the sexy older man who doesn't need Viagra and gets to bang beautiful young chicks half his age; he puts out his own line of videos called *Dave Cumming's Sugar Daddies.* Dave's business smarts also ensure that if any other directors needs an older man for a nonsexual role, like someone's father or a stuffy bank President, it is Dave Cummings who they call first.

Only recently have men begun to market and profit from their own images as actors. Probably the biggest, and most unexpected, male porn star success story is that of Jeff Stryker. Jeff is only one of two men featured in Leisure Time's mail-order ad in Penthouse for "200 Superstars of Video." He is the rare male porn star whose image sells videos, magazines, sexual aids, playing and greeting cards, calendars, T-shirts, CDs and even designer fashions. "Jeff Stryker's Realistic," a mass-marketed mold of his penis that is actually an inch longer than the real thing, is reportedly the top-selling specialty dildo. Marketed as a "luxury item," the cheapest one sells for $59.95. What's even more remarkable about Jeff's success is that the very first film he appeared in was a professional failure—a "stunt dick" had to be used because Jeff had problems getting wood. Not only that, Jeff started appearing in gay porn films before he crossed over successfully into straight films. His body was in such good shape when he entered gay porn that, between his first and second films, his fee went up from $3,000 to $13,500! By the time he shot his fourth film, producers were paying him upwards of $40,000. (Gay-porn actors usually are paid much better than straight-porn actors.) Instead of going straight up his nose in the form of cocaine, the money was put to good use building Jeff's sex-entertainment empire: he formed his own production company called Jeff Stryker Productions and his own line of products called "Jeff's Provisions." He now owns a sprawling house in the Hollywood Hills—with not one but two nannies for his son Joe—and 300 acres of land in rural Missouri with a 20-acre lake, on which Jeff built a 6,500 square foot ranch house with an all-marble bathroom. He plans to retire there when he finishes with porn.

G. Making Your Own

"If you can't beat 'em, join 'em," goes that old saying, and when it comes to breaking into porn, that ain't just whistling in the wind. Although entering the business through the normal route can sometimes be difficult, picking up a video camera can dramatically turn the equation in your favorite. After all, if you have a camera and some talent, and you capture the result on film, suddenly you aren't just a wannabe actor—you are a producer! If you can get the footage into some sort of professional looking shape, the only task that remains is finding someone to distribute your hot product. Remember, if you have a video *camera*, then you can have a video *company*, and if you have a video *company* then you can definitely have a video *business*. (Of course, you will want to check your local and state laws before doing anything. See *The Laws* section below.)

Take this success story as an example: a lonely, horny guy has no girlfriends, no money, and evidently no job. All he has to his name is a rundown apartment and a video camera. So what does he do? He cruises the streets of L.A. in one long booty call. Approaching cute girls, he shyly talks to them while videotaping them, then he offers to take them home to show them what kind of videos he makes. If the girl's curiosity is peaked, they go back to the guy's apartment where he shows her his videos. One thing leads to another until pretty soon she's dancing for him, stripping for him, and finally fucking him wildly. And the guy does not hold back. He gets the girl to do the most kinky, nasty sex acts imaginable. She takes it hard, deep and raw, and the guy obviously enjoys every second of it. Not only that, once he blows his wad with this chick, he simply goes back on the street and finds another one.

Who is this lucky guy? His name is Max Hardcore, one of the most successful porn directors in the world. Max handles his own casting, directing, filming and fucking. Prior to making his own films, Max had no connections and no experience, but his raunchy, authentic product caught the eye of Zane Entertainment, a big adult video company, who signed him to a contract and agreed to distribute his films. Now, his videos are humongous bestsellers, he travels the world with his own production company, Filmwest Productions, and pulls down a solid six-figure income. His films are intense "to the max"—hence, his name: Max Hardcore.

Costs. A big porn company like Vivid shoots eight new hardcore movies a month— half on video, half on 16mm film—with an average budget of $80,000. This is why Amateur or Gonzo porn is so popular amongst beginning filmmakers. A good amateur product can take only one to two days to shoot with a nominal budget of about $7,000 to $8,000. But don't expect to become a Max Hardcore or a Jeff Stryker overnight. It can take months or even years before you reap the rewards of your efforts. This is why you have to have a system already in place if you want to make money at porn.

Obviously, the first step is to get a video camera. For your initial project, almost any camera will do as long as you convey the air of a professional. Don't get hung up with wanting all the fanciest, most up-to-date equipment. These days, a half-decent camcorder sells brand-new for around $400; a used one goes for around $200. Excellent cameras can be had for under $1,000. The top-of-the-line camera is the BetaCam SP—a professional version of the BetaCam used by most regular folks—because of its superior picture-resolution and dub quality. It will also cost you about ten grand. These days, broadcast-quality digital cameras are becoming extremely reasonable, so you may want to investigate them as another alternative.

Fortunately, most of the newer models of cameras are of high quality and insanely easy to operate. One important feature to look for on your camera is its "zoom ratio," which is how far the lens will close in on your subject to capture all of the hot action you film. Also crucial is your camera's light sensitivity; many now come equipped with very sophisticated digital chips that make shooting indoors a breeze. Your camera should have a decent microphone to catch every coo and moan. Finally, you will need access to a basic editing system—typically two VCRs and an editing console so you can take two tapes and edit them into a master copy. Many companies distributing films in the "Amateur" market will take any tape in any format as long as it's hot and nasty and reasonably well put-together.

If you prefer not to purchase equipment right away, you can rent camera and/or editing equipment by the day. Photographic equipment is available for rental in almost every major city in the U.S. You can get a top-of-the-line package for just a few hundred bucks per day, and these will include lights, tripods, mikes, etc. Check your local Yellow Pages for rental companies and their rates.

Setting Up Shop. Before doing anything, as I mentioned earlier, you MUST check your local and state laws to make sure that adult film production is legal in your area. Assuming it is, you will need to follow all the proper procedures for starting a business. The authorities are going to want to see proof that you are a filmmaker and not a pimp. This is where setting up your own shop and leaving a nice, legal paper trail makes all the difference in the world. Take care of it now and not later.

There are four basic actions you have to undertake to start your business. The actual paperwork varies according to state and county, but the rules are essentially the same:

(1) File a fictitious business name statement with the county you plan to do business in, and publish the statement in a local newspaper. (See 'Choosing Your Name' section of this chapter.) Once you have a name for yourself or your business, you can go to almost any newspaper and ask them to file the statement for you. For a small fee, they'll take care of all

the work for you, including getting the proper forms from the county clerk as well as seeing if someone else is using the name already. The whole shebang should cost you about $100.

(2) Set up a DBA account at your local bank. DBA stands for "doing business as." You'll need to show the bank your fictitious business-name statement in order to set up the account. There are two important reasons for doing this: first, if you ever try to sell your video tapes you'll need to be able to cash checks made out to your business name; and second, you'll be able to keep track of your business expenses more easily. Not only will this make it simpler for you to claim tax deductions for all your expenses, but it will look professional to the authorities if your activities are ever called into question.

(3) Apply for a business license. This too involves a fee, which varies according to your location and the nature of your business. You will probably want to tell the clerk you are in the business of "video production." If you think you may want to do mail-order sales, you should mention that too. There may be a business tax in addition to or in substitution for the license.

(4) Register with the state board of equalization and apply for a seller's permit. If you plan to sell your videos directly to your customers, you must pay taxes on the gross receipts from these retail sales. Of course, you will be reimbursed by collecting this sales tax from your customers. Also, the seller's permit will allow you to avoid paying sales tax on items that you end up reselling (i.e., blank videotapes).

Once you complete these steps, you are a legal business. *It is crucial that you do not violate any tax laws!* This means filing accurate sales tax and income tax returns and reporting all sales, including those made in cash. If the local authorities want to try to bust your operation, the first approach they will always take is to see if you are violating any tax laws. Don't make the mistake so many other porn-makers have, which is to get sloppy on your taxes. A good accountant can be your pit bull against anyone trying to shut you down through your (perfectly legal) financial dealings. You should tell your accountants what you do for a living and make sure that they are okay with it.

Hanging Out Your Shingle. Now that you've obtained your camera and equipment and set up your business, you are ready to tell the world about your empire. Yes, there are a few steps for this as well:

(1) Get a voice-mail number. You should record a professional-sounding outgoing message (preferably with your new business name on it).

In most areas, voice-mail service runs from $5 to $10 a month. Service typically includes assigning you a new phone number that you can dedicate exclusively to your production efforts. Depending on what markets you recruit from, I also suggest you get a business mailing address, such as can be had from Mail Boxes Etc.

(2) Place a classified ad. This step is optional, as you may prefer to get your talent from Jim or Reb or another agent. If you do decide to place an ad, there are a million different ways to word it, depending on the market. The most common ad indicates that you are casting for an adult video. You may want to specify that nudity is involved. Make sure to include your voice-mail number in the ad.

(3) Interview your talent. Be totally up front to your performers that you are casting an adult video. Make sure they know exactly what is expected of them and that they are comfortable with your requirements. Tell your talent what you are willing to pay them. If they aren't interested, simply move on to your next interview.

As for what papers to advertise in, you have all sorts of choices: daily or weekly newspapers, college papers and X-rated papers. The adult newspapers are a good bet if you are looking for people who already have experience in the industry. These papers allow you to be a little more explicit because that's what they do. Sometimes a less explicit ad in a regular mainstream newspaper can also be successful. Mainstream papers offer you a bigger and more diverse talent pool. The important thing is to have a good, tasteful ad that emphasizes all the positives but is not in any way misleading. Just be patient when you are interviewing your talent. You will eventually find someone who suits your needs, but don't expect to find them overnight.

Stages of Production.

1. *Pre-production:* This is all the work that one has to take care of even before the actors arrive on the set or the camera is turned on. This is where the director and producer sit down and start making the decisions: "Do we write the script or do we hire a writer to do it?" or "Are we going to hire a whole crew or just use one camera?" Props have to be found, talent has to be hired, and locations have to be scouted.

Pre-production is also where working out a budget would be helpful. (It's better to know how much you have to spend before you start spending it, right?) A typical porn film budget could include a cameraman ($500 per day), a director ($400 per day) and, obviously, the male and female talent—men get around $400 and women, as we well know, can name their own price. $450-$600 is the usual starting rate for an untried girl, and it goes up from there. The key to making the most of your budget, whether it be big or small, is to have all the money you spend show up onscreen. In other words, the challenge of making porn is getting the most "bang for your buck."

One of the most critical parts of the pre-production process is obtaining the proper legal shooting permits. This, of course, depends on the laws on pornography that regulate your city and state. In Los Angeles, one of the few places where porn is legal to film, a filmmaker needs to call or go down to the Los Angeles Film Board. (See the Appendix for the office locations.) The L.A. Film Board doesn't care what kind of film you're shooting—they just want you to pay your $385 fee plus $85 for a fire marshal to spot check two locations. The film permit is valid for 14 days and up to 10 locations. Obtaining the permit also requires proof of $1 million of general liability insurance which covers performers, and crews as well as damage to equipment, automobiles or property. This costs about $1,500 a year.

The Shoot: As Nina Hartley told me, "Anything can go wrong on a porn shoot. It's always something." Just imagine the atmosphere on a shoot: the director is balancing a million different things, the performers are concerned with whether they're in the right mood, the cameraman is worried about his equipment. Things can get tense, hours long, and tempers short. Obviously, there is no substitute for experience, but a few basic rules can help guide even a novice shooter:

(a) *Don't use the autofocus while you're actually shooting or the focus will be constantly shifting. Instead, only use the autofocus to set the shot, then turn it off.*

(b) *Minimize zooming while you're shooting. Instead, use the zoom control to frame the shot before you start filming.*

(c) *Vary your shots by cutting to the image you want. Break things up by shifting from wide shots to medium shots to close-ups. Don't shoot from one angle for too long.*

For more details, you can always consult your instruction manual. You might even want to pick up a book on the subject. I recommend Kevin Campbell's *Video Sex.* The good news is that, no matter how crappy your initial product is, I guarantee someone else has made big bucks off something *even crappier.*

3. *Post-Production:* This is where you do your editing, pick your titles, add a music track, and get the completed film ready for reproduction. Post-production can take anywhere from one day to three weeks and can cost you between $300 and $3,000 for a fairly professional job. Before you even think of getting to this stage, make sure that all of your on-screen

performers have signed model release forms, or else they can sue you for using their images without their permission. (See a sample release in the Appendix). This is how strict the Law is about this point: even if you film yourself, and only yourself, on camera masturbating or doing whatever, you must give yourself a model release form to sign and keep on file! The best time to get the releases signed is before you start filming, but if you haven't secured them by the post-production stage, I wouldn't spend another nickel until you have them neatly tucked away in your possession.

Advertising. This is a fundamental part of selling any product—and porn videos are no different. Practically half of the industry's biggest trade magazine, *Adult Video News* (called "the Bible of X"), consists of advertisements. Any fledgling filmmaker has to compete with hundreds of other titles—*AVN* estimates there are maybe 10 big production companies in the Valley, 30 to 40 midlevel companies, and then 200 small companies constantly churning out product. It is important that you think up a good strategy to help sell your movie and let people know exactly what it is they're buying. Go check out the adult section of your local video store to do some comparison market research. Usually, porn advertisements stress the girl or girls who are starring in the movie. The popular style of late has been luxurious photographs, like pictures in lingerie catalogs. Although the biggies like Vivid or Wicked shoot all of their own boxcovers, there are a few companies in Los Angeles that specialize in advertising and boxcover design. Whatever ad campaign you decide to go with, I suggest you don't piss off your potential fans by featuring a girl on your boxcover or in your ad who is not in your movie—it's called false advertising.

Distribution. This is where the big money is made, and it's also probably the hardest nut to crack when you want to put out your own product. The way distribution works is fairly simple. A filmmaker delivers the master copy of film or video to the distributor in exchange for a cut of the product's profits from sales to different markets. Sometimes the filmmaker gets an upfront payment in addition to or instead of a percentage cut—that's up to you to negotiate. Once a deal is struck, the distributor usually is responsible for reproduction, packaging, and shipping costs. Of course, it is possible to distribute the film yourself. You can always start your enterprise as a mail-order company where you ship directly to customers. Alternatively, you can go to a broker who sells your movies to the distribution network of connections he has already made. For example, General Video of America is referred to as a "one-stop" distribution center. They deal in mostly amateur videos and sell directly to the retailer.

Keep in mind that there are many other markets for porn films besides adult video stores. Possible outlets include cable (domestic and foreign), CD-ROM, DVD, Internet, and mail-order. When you sit down to negotiate with a distributor, you should negotiate the rights for each of these markets separately. If you decide to set-up your own mail-order company, remember that you can always feel free to contact retailers yourself. A list of all the adult video stores in the country can be found in the index of the Adam World Film Guide's *Directory of Adult Films*. *[The directory is available at most adult bookstores or write Adam Film World, 8060 Melrose Avenue, Los Angeles, CA 90046-7082.*

1. *High-Tech Sex.* Once again, porn is on the forefront of cutting-edge technology. "In much the same way that hardcore films on videocassette were largely responsible for the rapid introduction of the VCR," reported *U.S. News & World Report,* "porn on CD-ROM and the Internet has hastened acceptance of these new technologies." Some of the more interesting meldings of sex and high-tech include a sort of virtual reality sex called "Cyberdildonics." This includes products like "robo-suck," in which a man can receive a virtual blowjob from a device plugged into his computer that is manipulated over the Web by a girl stripping for him halfway around the globe. Vivid Entertainment is developing something called a "cybersuit," which looks sort of like a transparent scuba outfit and gives men and women "full-body sexual workout" through being hooked up to, of all things, their printer drives. The possibilities are endless for marrying sex to New Media, but here are a few of the basic options you have:

(a) *The Internet:* Because of a glut of adult content online, you might not get much initial profit from setting up a website, but it can definitely act as a nice profile booster once you start making product. Actresses like Asia Carrera, Jill Kelly, Stacy Valentine and Mimi Miyagi have been doing very well with their websites and webcams. Lots of people are profiting exclusively off their sex websites, which people pay to access in very much the same way they do a phone sex line. Adult sex sites are taking in millions of dollars a month offering every form of voyeuristic pleasures. Check out Danni's Hard Drive on the Web (www.danni.com); this is a good example of a quality sex website that is doing terrific business. Websites belonging to Playboy and Penthouse now average about five million hits per day. The first step in setting up your website is to get your own sexy domain name, preferably one related to the name you filed as a DBA. Getting a domain name costs around $70. You will also need a company to host your website, which costs around $20 a month. You can find lists of web-hosting companies in the back of any Internet magazine. Just be sure to tell them that you plan to have adult content, and check your local and state laws to be sure that what you're doing is legal. The second step is putting together sexy material for your site. This can simply be nude photographs of yourself or anyone you hire to pose for your site. If you do that, you will need to obtain signed model release forms with proof that your talent is over 18 years of age, just like you would a normal porn video. Step #3 is to collect the money from your site, which can be done a number of different ways. You can get your own merchant account to accept credit cards, or you can sign up with one of the many age-verification companies that charge visitors a small fee to make sure they're legal. You in turn will get a piece of this fee, and the dollars can start adding up once your traffic picks up. Just be sure to follow the usual promotional steps of registering with the major search engines, trading links and banners with other webmasters and webmistresses—like yours truly!—and putting in the proper key words and metatags in your HTML code. (If this sounds like ancient Greek, just go to www.infoseek.com and they will explain it to you on their submission page.)

(b) CD-ROM: This format allows a multimedia experience of images, speech, text, music and video clips. CD-ROMs such as *Virtual Valerie* and *The Penthouse Photo Shoot* created interest in multimedia equipment amongst the buying public mainly because the user can interact and affect the action onscreen: *Virtual Valerie*, which is also available in a bondage version called *Donna Matrix*, remains one of the most popular porn-related CD-ROMs because a man can bring Valerie or Donna to orgasm by using his computer mouse's point-and-click feature. There are currently three version of CD-ROMs on the market: photographic stills, movies and interactive games. The games in particular seem to be set for a long-term market because of the constant innovations being brought to the genre. The best thing about technology like CD-ROMs is that you don't even need to make new images: You can simply lift scenes from your existing images. *Fuckout*, for example, contains material from other hardcore porn movies. The capacity to repackage and resell old material is, to pardon the pun, "virtually unlimited."

(c) DVD: This format is being hyped as the next territory for adult entertainment—almost all of the new personal computers will include DVD drives. Studios like Vivid are releasing two DVD titles a week. The appeal of DVD technology is that it can hold more data and process it more quickly than CD-ROM.

2. *Cable.* After rental videos, satellite and cable television are the next biggest markets for porn films. Vivid Entertainment provides 80% of the softcore porn films that appear on Playboy's popular cable channel. Vivid has also launched a new pay-per-view cable service called AdultVision that offers porn films around the clock. Other X-rated cable shows include Spice, Pink, Electric Blue and The Girls of Penthouse. Some hardcore

channels are Exotic, Exxxtasy, and True Blue. The foreign and domestic cable markets include straight cable channels like Cinemax and HBO (which only are allowed to show softcore porn) as well as adult pay-per-view channels for major hotel chains. Pay-per-view in particular has become a large source of profits for cable companies. In 1996, Americans spent about $175 million to view porn in their rooms at major hotel chains such as Sheraton, Hilton, Hyatt and Holiday Inn. Another market that has recently started to become a viable alternative to the big-budget cable channels is public access. Public access shows do not have the types of restrictions that normal TV channels have, and thus the content can be a little more racy. (Standards for what you can show on public access vary according to state and local laws, however.) Some popular porn-related public access shows include Al Goldstein's *Midnight Blue* and *The Robin Byrd Show* out of New York, and *Colin's Sleazy Friends* and Dr. Susan's Block's *Sex Talk* out of Los Angeles. These shows, have become cult favorites and feature interviews with porn stars. Even if you don't feel like hosting your own show, an appearance on one of the established cable-access programs couldn't hurt to get your image out there to the public.

3. *Features.* Despite the death of porn on 35mm film, big-budget videos are still being made. In fact, the budgets for movies like *Conquest* and *Zazel* ran upwards of $200,000, an industry record. Most porn features are filmed in three to five days, whereas low-budget films require just a day or two. But keep in mind that porn features, like big-time MTV videos, are what you make after you've climbed your way to the top of the directing, acting or producing pool.

4. *Gonzo/Amateur.* In 1989, a bold director named John Stagliano revolutionized porn with *The Adventures of Buttman*. His approach was simply to walk around his house with a video camera as he filmed his 'friends' having sex. Since there was no staging or storyline, Stagliano was able to radically reduce costs, but viewers went crazy for his realistic approach. Soon enough, other porn directors caught on and his style of filming was dubbed "Gonzo."

The downside of the Gonzo revolution is that everybody and their mother realized they just needed a video camera and some model release forms to make a porn video. One of the few truly accurate parts about the film *Boogie Nights* was its depiction of how the explosion of amateur video porn killed off a lot of careers of the old timers who had been in the business since the 70s. Gonzo films now make up more than 50% of the porn market and show no signs of slowing down. "Amateur" video is a huge subgenre of the Gonzo market. Alongside Gonzo, it exploded in the mid-80s due to the high number of everyday people, mostly couples, who would send in tapes they made of themselves having sex in hopes of breaking into the business. The reasons why it's so popular are simple: it's cheap, it's easy, it's acceptable and anybody can do it. "Besides," Nina Hartley told me, "the enthusiasm of the amateur performer is not to be believed. They are actually liking what they are doing! They actually fucking act! They look like real people you can meet in real life!"

In addition to General Video of America, there are a number of accessible companies that distribute amateur porn: Tim & Alyssa Lake's San Diego-based Homegrown Video offers more than 500 different tapes of ordinary people having sex. The company pays the "stars" $20 for every minute of video it uses—about half the tapes Homegrown receives are eventually released. Like Homegrown, most of the companies that distribute amateur porn are located in Southern California, but there are hardcore amateur-video companies distributing tapes in Ohio, Missouri, Kansas, Illinois and Tennessee. Nina Hartley recommends two amateur distributors whom she has found helpful and trustworthy: St. Louis's Video Alternatives (1-800-444-8336), which accepts standard porn fare, and San Francisco's Good Vibrations (1-415-974-8980), which distributes more adventurous porn specialty videos.

5. *Fetish/Specialty.* There are so many subgenres to this market it could take up a whole chapter just listing them. Take foot fetishes, for example: there are markets for bare feet, feet in high-heels, feet with brown stockings, feet with black stockings, smelly feet, clean feet, feet with long toenails, feet with painted toenails—you name it, there's someone out there who likes to watch it.

Specialty videos vary as much as people's sexual desires. Subjects include older women and younger men, younger men and older women, fat women, straight women and gay men, girl-wrestling, striptease, nail fetishes, women or men getting dressed or undressed, catfights, men masturbating alone, interracial sex, women putting on lipstick or smoking, men with long hair, women with hairy legs, toys, leather, women in high-heels, performers who look like celebrities, women in Nazi uniforms, "sex balloonists" (don't ask), light spanking, bondage and S&M, mud fights, food fights, women trying on shoes, tall women, tall men, dwarves—the list for specialties is positively endless. And so is the opportunity to create and profit from your own market, or "specialty."

6. *Gay/Bi/Lesbian/Transsexual.* These are similar but distinct sub-categories of porn. Typically, "gay" means men having sex with men. "Bi" means women having sex with men who are bisexual. "Lesbian" has two types of films under its umbrella: women making love to women in films made specifically for the lesbian market, and women making love to women for the benefit of a male audience. There are also two types of transsexuals who appear in porn: "preops," who have done everything to

change themselves into a woman except have a sex-change operation; and "postops" who have gone that extra few inches. And surprise: transsexuals have their own subgenre of films, including S&M and Hispanic. You see? In porn, everybody, if you pardon the expression, "makes out."

As I mentioned earlier, gay porn is it's own separate industry with its own rules and regulations. Suffice it to say that along with "specialty" and "fetish" videos, the unexploited possibilities are enormous. For example, many heterosexual women who rent porn prefer to rent gay movies—not only because gay porn often features better looking men but because it's a chance for a woman to watch good looking men getting off without the interference of a woman. (Not all women have lesbian tendencies!) And yet, *virtually no one has made any films for this untapped market.* The opportunity to cross genre boundaries, very much like John Stagliano did with his films, can be a chance for you to make a name for yourself as someone who truly innovated the world of X.

7. *Couples.* A burgeoning new genre in porn involves catering to couples who want to experience a sex video but don't want all the hardcore sleaze. Women like Candida Royale and Joanna Williams were the pioneers of what is now called "couples cinema." Paul Thomas is probably the most successful director working at it right now. Couples movies can include not just dramatic narratives but instructional sex videos like *How To Put the Romance Back in Your Life, The Couple's Guide To Light Spanking* or *Fun Bedroom Games, Volume 1: Role–Playing.* You can also instruct people on using yoga or tantric sex to increase their sexual enjoyment. The market is deep and wide for this type of genre; Adam & Eve out of North Carolina is one of the biggest companies that deals in instructional materials for couples. As with anything, there is a good and bad side to the couples genre. The good side is that you can cloak hot and erotic sex in the guise of instructing people, which may protect you more from anyone wishing to put you out of business because you are producing "educational materials." The bad side is that most couples cinema falls into the softcore category, which is often much more expensive to produce for a beginning filmmaker. But, it can be done.

The Law. Rules and regulations vary from region to region, and they constantly change even in the same region, which is why you absolutely must check your state and local laws before you do anything in the world of X. I'm not a lawyer nor can I give legal advice, so I can only provide some common sense guidelines and precautions:

(1) Do not videotape or involve minors in any of your business activities. Make sure all your actors and actresses provide you with valid proof of their age. Keep copies of this proof on file forever. Have all your talent sign professional model release forms, wherein they admit to

understanding that they will be involved in an adult videotape produced for sale and distribution, and that they are signing away all rights to this videotape. [A sample form is provided in the Appendix.]

(2) Do not videotape anyone without their knowledge or permission. Even in areas considered public domain, like the beach or the streets, it is always better to ask people for their consent first.

(3) Do not force, persuade or threaten anyone to participate in your videos. This is common sense. You don't want your actors or actresses to later accuse you of taking advantage of them.

(4) Know where your material is at all times. Someone who gets hold of your tapes or footage can either rip you off or try to get you in trouble with Mr. Law. If you've made a tape you're not sure is legal, DESTROY OR ERASE IT!

(5) Do not mix extreme bondage or S&M scenes with hardcore sex. The government considers S&M videos to be depictions of violence and not just "acting" or "role-playing." Combining hardcore sex and S&M spells sex that has been forced on someone against their will in the eyes of any prosecuting attorney. Make sure you are familiar with the codes and forms of legal films of this sort.

(6) Do not make videos that depict urination, defecation, fisting, or sex with animals. These sort of videos can get you in a lot of trouble, so my recommendation is that you steer clear of them.

(7) Do not use copyrighted music as a background for your videos. If you do, you are legally responsible to pay residuals on it. This is where you can ask your music pals to let you use their demos tape instead, or else compose an original score "for fun." You might also film your hardcore scenes with no music at all, as most X-rated film aficionados prefer as little distractions as possible.

(8) Require all your actors and actresses to have regular and updated tests for HIV/AIDS and other sexually-transmitted diseases. This not only increases the safety factor (as well as the talents' comfort level), but also decreases your liability in the event that one of your male or female employees contracts a nasty virus.

I suggest you consult a lawyer who will clarify any questions you have about these issues, as well as inform you of other legal precautions you have to take. There are many good attorneys who are involved and well-versed in legal issues of adult entertainment. For instance, Jeffery Douglas (1-310-576-3411) specializes in criminal defense and First Amendment issues; and Allan Gebhard (1-818-386-9200) is an expert in civil and intellectual-property law.

There are also a couple of legal resource services that can help you on a more general basis. The Legal Resource Center (1-818-380-6866) is located near the offices of World Modeling, P.A.W. and AIM, and it offers self-help legal services and document preparation. The Legal Grind Coffee & Counsel (1-800-GRIND-95) is both a coffee shop and bonafide law research and referral center offering $20 legal advice over creamy mochas and yummy pastries. There are two locations of the Legal Grind, one in Santa Monica (2640 Lincoln Boulevard; 1-310-452-8160) and one in the San Fernando Valley community of Tarzana (19221 Ventura Boulevard; 1-818-342-3405). Only in L.A.!

3

The Resources

(AS IN: "WHAT IS OUT THERE FOR ME?")

"The family of X can only protect itself from within."
—Bill Margold

John Stagliano, one of the most influential porn directors of the last decade, once announced to the press that "the hardcore industry is disease free." Not long after he said this, Stagliano's girlfriend, porn actress Krysti Lynn, took his white Acura on Los Virgenes Canyon Road, which connects Malibu to the San Fernando Valley. Driving at around 100 mph, Lynn lost control of the car and slid across a dirt shoulder before plunging down a 30-foot ravine. The bodies of Lynn and her female passenger weren't discovered until 48 hours later. In a moment of "depression-fueled weakness," Stagliano had unprotected anal sex with a Brazilian transsexual prostitute. In the Spring of 1997, he tested positive for the HIV virus.

Stagliano has not contracted full-blown AIDS, but his unfortunate circumstance demonstrates a lot of the myths and realities of contracting HIV from the porn industry. First, Stagliano contracted the virus from someone *outside* the industry, rather than from an actress on set; second, his case was not hushed or covered up but announced almost immediately; and third and most important, Stagliano took it like a man and didn't, like so many before him, blame the Industry for catching the virus. In fact, American pornographers take more care to protect themselves and their employees than their peers in Europe and Asia. Once the threat of AIDS became clear in the mid-to late 80s, the adult industry moved to reduce it as fast as possible. Producers began to insist on the use of condoms, and now performers have to undergo an AIDS test once a month and provide proof that they are clean before anyone will employ them.

It's not 100% foolproof, but it has kept the hardcore industry relatively AIDS-free.

Of course, there have been casualties, the most high-profile being actor John Holmes, director Chuck Vincent and actress Lisa DeLeeuw. Yet their deaths have been related to their activities offscreen rather than on. Holmes, for example, had serviced both male and female clients as a male prostitute for years and was also a major drug user. Most of the other porn stars to die of AIDS tended to be male performers like Marc Stevens, Wade Nichols or R.J. Reynolds, who had either starred in gay porn films or had gay relationships outside the Industry, and were in high-risk groups because of their lifestyles. In fact, the truth is that AIDS has decimated gay porn. Over 100 gay performers have died since the 1980s. Due to this catastrophe, however, gay porn is now the safest genre of the business.

To this date, no exclusively heterosexual porn performer has died of AIDS. Still, it should be known that a second outbreak has occurred in hetero porn. At least eight females and two males have tested HIV-positive in the last two years, including Marc Wallice, Nena Cherry, Kimberly Jade, Jordan McKnight, Caroline, Brooke Ashley and Tricia Devereaux. Marc Wallice is widely thought to be 'Patient Zero,' or the source of the infection, having engaged on-camera in unprotected anal sex with the infected girls. Both Wallice and Cherry were also intravenous drug users, but the recent outbreak has also coincided with a disturbing new trend in hetero porn—a return to unprotected, often anal, sex. This is a result of the fact that most porn fans and viewers do not like to see condoms used in their porn because it ruins the sexual fantasy with the reminder of AIDS and disease. Porn makers have responded in kind, giving the public exactly what it wants whether it is courting death or not; many performers, especially the newer ones, are all too ready to comply, thinking that having an AIDS test is enough protection without the condom. Bill Margold, in particular, is disturbed by the trend of porn girls who go off to work at legal brothels in Nevada. "We fought all these years to prove we're not whores," he says, "and now these kids are going to drag us right back down where we came from." Bill sees a day when the X-rated industry could be shut down as a public health risk.

Many of porn's top actresses have retired because of the threat of AIDS, including Hypatia Lee, Annette Haven and Asia Carrera. And despite the precautions and the founding of AIM, the first-ever health-care foundation for the performers of the adult film industry, the fear that adult stars are playing Russian Roulette with their bodies persists. This chapter provides some basic information and resources so you can weigh for yourself the risks intrinsic to the world of porn.

A. HEALTH STANDARDS AND PRACTICES

Testing. Because of the threat of sexually-transmitted diseases (STDs) in porn, and because of the recent HIV outbreak in 1998, the adult industry has made great strides to contain the spread of HIV and to notify the industry of infected performers. Although condoms are not required, a blood test for HIV and other STDs is. Every production requires its talent to bring an *original copy* of their most recent HIV test. All performers are required to get a new HIV test *every 30 days*. (Gay porn productions require an AIDS test every two weeks.) What this means is that if your last test is 31 days old you will not be permitted to perform. In some cases, especially with HIV/AIDS and its six month gestation period (the amount of time it takes for HIV to show up in the blood), producers are extra careful and require that you begin testing up to six months *before* you even make your first film.

Unlike condoms, there is no stigma attached to testing. If anything, it is seen as a courtesy and a sign of your good faith that you would consider and be concerned with your co-workers. As a performer, you have the right to refuse to work with anyone with an outdated test. If you do decide to work with them anyway, with or without condoms, it'll be just that: your decision.

AIM Health Care Foundation. The Adult Industry Medical Health Care Foundation (AIM) is a nonprofit medical clinic open five and a half days a week. AIM offers PCR/DNA testing for HIV as well as testing for other STD's like Hepatitis A, B and C—not to mention other medical services like pap smears, cosmetic surgery information, alternative health and healing methods, and support groups to deal with abuse or other emotional traumas.

What makes AIM special is that it is specifically for people in the sex industry. Where Bill Margold's Protecting Adult Welfare (P.A.W.) can help prepare and even heal your mind, Sharon Mitchell's AIM can help preserve and heal your body. Sharon was inspired to open up AIM after the 1998 HIV outbreak amongst several porn males and females. The outreach services offered by AIM include:

1) *Drug and pregnancy testing.*
2) *Continued certified counseling and aftercare for people who are HIV positive.*
3) *Drug & alcohol rehabilitation, placement and in-house certified counseling.*
4) *Special scheduled doctors to provide other health care opportunities.*
5) *Peers who offer their special talents: i.e., physical trainers, yoga, alternative health care providers and how-to instructors.*

6) *Support groups for both male and female talent, as well as 12-step meetings.*
7) *Informative brochures and videos on all related health concerns for adult performers.*

AIM is staffed with expert counselors, nurse practitioners, phlebotomists (people legally trained and licensed to draw blood), psychiatrists, chiropractors and other health-care professionals who offer a friendly, casual attitude while giving you the most up to date testing and information available to keep you healthy in an often unhealthy business. The most important service of AIM is the testing it does for the Human Immunodeficiency Virus (HIV), of which it offers a variety of types. The three most well-known tests are:

1) *The ELISA (or "enzyme-linked immunosorbent assay") test is part of a group of tests that are used to screen people for HIV by looking for antibodies in human blood. This simple test is usually the first one used to check for both HIV and Hepatitis C (HCV).*

2) *The 'Western Blot' test is a follow-up test usually done after an ELISA test has come back positive for HIV antibodies.*

3) *The PCR/DNA (or a "viral load") test measures the amount of HIV virus in the blood. It is probably the most sophisticated and accurate of all the HIV/AIDS tests and is the preferred test for all sex workers.*

You can also get tested for AIDS and other STD's at any legitimate medical clinic—there is another popular testing center in North Hollywood. Keep in mind, AIM is not just a clinic but a counseling spot, a crash pad, a sort of clubhouse and congregating area for porn talent. It's right around the corner from Jim South's World Modeling Agency and Bill Margold's P.A.W. offices. Since AIM is a nonprofit organization, they are not interested in taking money from you. (See the Appendix for contact information for AIM and other testing centers.)

Common problems. Believe it or not, AIDS and Hepatitis are not the most common ailments that can befall a porn star. For women, Chlamydia, yeast infections, and pulled thigh muscles are probably the biggest complaints. Nonspecific urethritis is the most prevalent problem for the men. "Getting it up and keeping it up for up to two hours at a time is an unnatural thing for the penis," explains "Dr." Bill Margold, "because what happens is that the urethra lining starts to lubricate. But after a while it figures there's no reason to *keep* lubricating so it starts to dry up. And it causes flaking and that puts a strain on all the little capillaries running into the urethra. It's from staying hard too long. Male performers now aren't required to stay as hard as they used to because video-tape is cheap."

What To Do. Many companies and talent attempt to hastily "reconcile" their health records only after they complete a sex shoot. Considering this unacceptable, AIM has stepped in to keep tabs for all the involved parties. Sharon Mitchell, who runs AIM, suggests the following health advice for various participants in X-rated films:

> *Talent:* "Look at your partners' tests and make sure they are current: 30 days from the date their (and your) blood was drawn."

> *Directors:* "When you hire talent, ask them if they have a current PCR/DNA Test and let them know it is a necessity if they want to be in your film."

> *Producers/Production Managers:* "Let your talent know that there is a requirement of a current test on the day of the shooting."

> *Companies:* "Protect your liability. Have a one paragraph HIV policy in writing that states you are in possession of HIV records for talent upon shooting, before shooting, or upon payment."

Condoms. Condoms are still optional in porn but are mandatory in many of the bigger and more high-end productions. Despite complaints that they don't feel good or that they look unnatural, condoms are becoming more common and more accepted. The older porn performers started their careers before condoms were commonly used, so they are predictably a little reluctant to "suit up" as they say, whereas the newer generations of porn men and women who grew up with the AIDS scare have gotten so used to condoms that using them is just second nature. To be quite honest, it's not the condom that matters but the heat generated by the actors themselves that will make any viewer forget about all that rubber in the way.

The AIM Health Care Clinic has an extensive computer database called the Industries Test Clearinghouse, which cross-references each actor or actress's health preference for their partners: "Condom Only," "Condom Optional," or "No Condom." There are still companies that don't use condoms—evidently, they believe that people don't want to see sex with condoms onscreen, or they fear that they won't get a distribution deal, or perhaps they simply don't care. Being a safe-sex maven, I cannot comfortably endorse those companies. It is my advice that you always insist on the use of condoms and stay away from those who don't. Many male performers also wash with germicide cleansers before and after sex, and every good stud urinates immediately after having sex with someone.

Female Contraception. The diaphragm, with its various accompanying spermicides, is the most recommended contraception for female sex workers. Devices like Norplant or the birth-control pill are chemicals you put into your body but can't necessarily take out—and each react differently with different women's bodies. Another option is the "female condom," which looks sort of a diaphragm crossed with a rubber glove. I haven't met any girls who have used the female condom, nor guys who have been on the business end of them, so I don't feel qualified to comment on them. For women who don't like male or female condoms, there is a new product being tested through AIM called "Chemical Barrier Protection" which is like a spermicide. It is not approved by the Food & Drug Administration, but it reportedly has a 99% kill rate of STDs. In no way should it be a substitute for condoms, but this protection is better than nothing if you are a performer or director who shys away from rubbers.

Terminology. The world of HIV and other STD's is much too complicated to explain within the space allowed in this book, but there are a few terms whose definitions you should be aware of even before you walk into AIM or any other clinic:

AIDS (or Acquired Immune Deficiency Syndrome): A group of diseases that weakens the body's immune system and suppresses the body's ability to fight against disease. A person suffering from AIDS can die of a cold as well as a serious infection. Currently, there is no cure for AIDS.

Antibody: A protein created by the body's immune system to fight infections. Antibodies are paralyzed in a body infected with HIV.

Asymptomatic: This means a person who is carrying HIV but who shows no symptoms of the infection. It is possible to infect others, even if one is asymptomatic.

High Risk: This refers to sexual or drug-related activities that increase one's chances of contracting or transmitting HIV. The two most high-risk activities are having sex without using protection and the sharing of intravenous (I.V.) needles in drug use. Porn actors are considered a 'high-risk' category.

HIV (or Human Immunodeficiency Virus): HIV is the virus that causes AIDS. HIV is transmitted through activity that allows the blood, semen or vaginal fluid of one person to contact the blood or mucous membranes (in the eyes, mouth, vagina, or rectum) of another person. People who are "HIV Positive" carry the virus but have not contracted full-blown AIDS. It is not yet proven that all persons infected with HIV will develop AIDS.

Immune System: Specialized cells and proteins that make up a whole network of defense systems to guard the human body from infections.

Safe Sex: Practices that offer protection from HIV transmission during sex. These include condoms, plastic wrap or dental dams for oral sex, latex gloves or finger cots, female condoms and chemical barriers, vaginal spermicides in the form of foams, creams and jellies, etc.

Seroconversion: When someone's blood changes from having no HIV antibodies (called "seronegative") to having HIV antibodies (called "seropositive"). This usually, but not always, occurs within six months of exposure to the HIV virus.

Symptoms: Initial HIV symptoms are very similar to that of the flu: fever, swollen glands, sore throat, diarrhea, nausea, vomiting and red or dark skin rashes.

T-Cell: A type of white blood cell (also called a "lymphocyte") that is vital to the functioning of the immune system.

B. PORN PROFILE: AN INTERVIEW WITH SHARON MITCHELL

It was dark in her apartment. Sharon Mitchell remembers waking up with a throat full of blood and just one thought: "My God, I am going to die." She was not only being raped by a man who had forced his way into her apartment when she refused to have sex with him for money, she was being eaten by him. Literally. He had already shattered her larynx and was biting and chewing off pieces of her flesh. He was about to do much worse when Sharon got "that surge of adrenaline that everyone talks about." She fought a good 14 to 15 minutes for her life. She managed to position her assailant next to her weight pile. As she pulled the weight up and brought it down, she thought, "Well, fuck it, if it falls on me at least I die by my own hand." Luckily, it hit him. Sharon had to have reconstructive surgery to eliminate the teeth marks on her body. She was the lucky one: Police later found out that her assailant had already murdered two other women.

This was the turnaround for Miss Sharon Mitchell, or "Mitch", as practically everybody calls her now. After her near-death experience, she engaged in a little reconstructive surgery of the soul: first by counseling troubled young performers at Bill Margold's Protecting Adult Welfare (who she credits with "saving my fucking life") and then by founding the Adult Industry Medical Health Care Foundation.

In her 2,000-film history as a 25-year veteran of the X-rated industry, Mitch never engaged in anal sex and still became the first female porn star to receive $1,000 a day. She was also a serious heroin addict during the dangerous years before people knew of a disease called AIDS. Ironically, she directed **Dick of Death**, *a porn film about a guy who killed women by masturbating on them, which came out around the same time that HIV/AIDS started to become a national health concern. Mitch shot it like a horror movie. ("That was my cocaine period," she says. "I was very creative!") She has not written her autobiography yet because a lot of the pieces of the puzzle are still falling into place. "I had blackouts for decades," she said, "and they're getting more definitive." To see the 1984 documentary* **Kamikaze Hearts**, *which documented Sharon's heroin addiction as well as her destructive relationship with another porn starlet, is to see a woman who knows she is going to die soon and doesn't seem to care.*

Sharon Mitchell is porn's icon of courage and dedication.

ANA LORIA: *So Mitch, why aren't you dead?*

MITCH: *[Laughs loudly]* Because I'm not supposed to be! I'm one of those people who has just had a tumultuously interesting life. I started out in New York in a lot of legitimate stuff, like game shows and fashion shoots. Then I got involved with drugs and alcohol. When I started in porn years ago, it was really interesting because everyone in it was out-of-work actors or actresses, and we were all able to work on our normal lives during the day. I remember I had this modeling interview, and I was so fuckin' stoned; I had my modeling and acting portfolio in one hand and a bag of dildos in the other, and I sat down in front of the casting directors and took out the wrong bag—the one full of dildos. "Oops, wrong one!"

ANA: *But AIDS and related health problems are the reason you are here right now. With your intravenous drug use and all that, how did you manage to escape when so many other didn't?*

MITCH: I didn't share needles often. But I did in a couple of cases. When you're a junkie, you're gonna get desperate, because there are two guarantees with addiction: you're gonna run out, and you're gonna want more. I'm sure at one point that happened to me. I put myself in a lot of scary situations, and I honestly don't know how I got away with it. Everybody has their own journey in life, and everyone has their own path. I had the drugs, the alcohol, the sex, the travel, the stardom. I need to make this clear right off the bat, though: I do not blame the porn business for my addiction.

ANA: *Unlike a lot of other people...*

MITCH: Right. I had alcoholism in my family, and I sort of grew up around that. And being a little lonely and repressed, the porn industry was the perfect place for me to rebel. I think it was a natural thing for people of that time to experiment with drugs. That was New York in the 70s—the era of the Mudd Club, Plato's Retreat, CBGB's, and Max's Kansas City.

ANA: *I always associate New York porn with the grainy, exploitative, peep-show, raincoat crowd, and L.A. porn with the glamorous, beautiful side of the business. Is that a big misconception?*

MITCH: Well, you're talking about decades of change there. In 1975, the first adult movies I ever did had these huge budgets that are unheard of nowadays—I mean, hundreds of thousands of dollars! I had to wait *two years* for my first film to come out. I really actually had to wait before I could go into a theater and see one of my movies. Seeing my pussy sixteen feet high on a screen was a very thrilling thing for me. Some of those "grainy" 16mm loop things were actually fun to film. They were all shot on short-end in places like Central Park. We would just have so much fun.
I was always open about my drug use. I even worked it into my image.

It kind of worked for me in a way, and the industry perpetuated me as an addict. It kept me from doing a lot of the stuff that most addicts have to do. Because of the massive amounts of money I was making, it was facilitating my drug habit. It's a very dangerous mix: large ego, low self-esteem, lots of money. You're traveling all over the world. You go shopping in Paris and hang out with the French Hells' Angels—it's like being in a candy store! This was like the life of a princess. It was a life I don't think I ever could have asked for. I have great memories, I really do. I went for a really long time. It worked for me. I don't know. I tend not to ask why, because then I find myself in existential hell.

But I do know that the journey of pornography has been all-inclusive in my life. I mean, I'm sitting in my 25th year in this industry, and I've really gotten the chance to pave the way for a lot of women, as have my sisters Candida Royale, Veronica Hart, Vanessa Del Rio, Kelly Nichols, Marilyn Chambers, Gloria Leonard, Annie Sprinkle—I mean these are women who I am privileged to rub shoulders with. We even had our first support group together. It was called 'Club 90.' We would exchange lingerie and talk about our feelings and what it was like to be in the Industry.

ANA: *You were involved in porn back when it was still "illegal." Yet, even in the 90s, porn still has a certain social stigma attached to it.*

MITCH: There was a time when *[being in]* porn was a way to rebel. I thought, "Well, fuck it. I'm gonna be a fuckin' porno star!" I can say fuck you to the Catholic Church, my mother, the woman who was my real mother who abandoned me as a child, plus feed my ego and make tons of money. I mean, what a perfect combination for someone who needed a lot of attention. I think the stigma is there because we choose it. Part of what we want to be known for is being the bad girls and boys. On the other hand, I don't think anybody would terribly mind being praised for what they do, because in this day and age, it's a career. Today, you can actually say "I want to grow up to be a stripper and a porn star!" They can come down to AIM Healthcare and pick up the instruction tape for newcomers, they can take a seminar from Nina Hartley out here or Candida Royale in the East. They can take HIV 101 with me at Mission Community College. I mean, you can't get any more mainstream than that!

ANA: *You mentioned that AIM Health Care is at a critical stage in its development. What did you mean by that?*

MITCH: Because I'm taking it to another level. I had to fight like crazy from within and without the Industry to create and save this facility and the nature of what we do here. AIM originally started under [Bill Margold's] Protecting Adult Welfare and the Free Speech Coalition, which as we know is a group of manufacturers with other interests—primarily not for the talent, primarily not for health and welfare. The FSC is only willing to go so far. In other words, when this industry has an HIV crisis and we had to get our hands dirty, yes they coughed up a tremendous amount of money to start a testing facility—not even a facility, they just wanted to start a program. This was January 1998 on up. Clearly we were in the middle of a crisis: people were giving it to each other, it was clear it was coming in from the outside. We needed to find a solution, and I was sitting on the board of directors and they asked me to help. I had just finished my first credential as a chemical dependency specialist and HIV counselor, so I had all the resources to go with it. At that time, I had been doing a research paper for a class on the adult industry about how many people got tested and how many people didn't—and it was *bad*. It was very bad. The stats were like 13% of people got tested with the Elisa test *maybe* every six months. Just totally unacceptable.

ANA: *You actually publicly denounced the Elisa Tests at a FSC meeting.*

MITCH: Right. Elisa is bunk. Of course it is. I'm not saying that it doesn't work for certain amounts of people, but Elisa, along with the rule of 'private disclosure' [i.e., anonymous testing], is the basis for the fuckin' disease in this country. And I can say that because I have over 7,000 tests, and only a few positives. I have a solution that works by monitoring. What myself and Dr. York have created with input from various HIV researchers, scientists and microbiologists is a fuckin' system that works. Period.

ANA: *What's the difference between the Elisa Test and the PCR/DNA test?*

MITCH: The primary difference is that the Elisa test has a window period of six months. Now, that test measures for the antibody levels. In other words, when that antibody becomes positive we call that 'sero-conversion,' which means it's affected the antibodies of the blood and we're able to detect it that way, right? That could take up to six months in a normal, healthy person—just the type of people who work in the porn industry. So, if we're going by that test, and people are working with 40 sex partners a month, and those sex partners are working with 40 other people a month... with all the shooting that goes on in the San Fernando Valley, think of how much infection could go on with anonymous testing. So, this is the model for what didn't work. We know it didn't work. Why? Because we got all the HIV in the industry. It had permeated the industry regardless of who's who and what's what.

Now, the PCR/DNA test scans for the HIV inhibitor only. And when it fits in and inhibitors are found, that's detected before 'sero-conversion,' meaning we detect the virus very, very early. Sometimes within

10 days. When we find people that are positive by this test, we do a con-firmatory test. We're talking *early* detection, sometimes within 2-6 weeks. Meanwhile, they take the Elisa Test and still come out negative. In every single case. I'm not saying the Elisa Test is worthless. It does some good for people who maybe have cheated on their wife in the last 33 years, but not for this industry. Because, effectively, if we use PCR/DNA every 30 days, which is what we do. We test between 300 to 400 people every 30 days. We are not about anonymous testing, we are about 'partner disclo-sure.' When someone becomes positive, we sit that person down and make a list of who they've worked with. We double-check it with the manufacturers that support us and donate money to us, to make sure we have our figures right. We notify all the people that they've worked with. We then hit the button in the database and can tell who's worked with whom, who falls into the window period of exposure. Then we put them on 'quarantine'. We make them count 21 days from when they last worked with anyone—we find them other work in editing or being a P.A. and just tell them to sit tight—and then we retest them. Then they can be released back into the Industry. That's an effective way to monitor dis-ease.

The PCR/DNA is a non-FDA proved test, which means we don't use it as diagnostic, but we do use it as monitoring. In other words, if some-one comes up positive on the PCR/DNA, we use it as an alert to contin-ue with the other confirmatory tests—like the Western Blot, which meas-ures all the *[virus]* proteins—the *last* of which is the Elisa Test. So I would do a PCR/DNA test, a Western Blot, an Elisa and an RNA, which meas-ures the viral load. So by then we can really judge.

ANA: *So was the split between AIM and the Free Speech Coalition over these tests?*

MITCH: It was over the liability, my dear. The manufacturers didn't want to deal with the liability, but they aren't risking anything. It's us—the actors—who have literally *everything* to lose. I lost my fuckin' mind because I sat on the FSC's Board of Directors, who basically handed me on a silver platter to help find a solution and worked with me for that solu-tion, and I felt a lot of solidarity there. I did it within the guise of P.A.W., which really wasn't prepared. It was kind of a mom 'n' pop, huggy-bear, peer-counseling service, and they are wonderful for what they do. But when I'm sitting here with my health credentials, a purpose or cause, the anxiety of just being a couple years clean at that time, the anger that I had in me in my core issues towards the manufacturers. There was a time when I wanted to blame this industry for my addiction, and all these little bits and particles really fueled my purpose and my sense of being. I thought, "How perfect! I can actually start my new life here as a coun-selor, clinician, and eventually, a doctor." So I told [the Free Speech Coalition] that I really wanted to do it, and they said, "No! You have to stop! You can't do this under the guise of the FSC." Again, they didn't want the liability. They were so afraid if I were to make a mistake or a misdiagnosis or whatever, then they would lose all their fortune. And that, my dear, is more important to some people than human life. That's just the way the world works.

So we're at a stalemate here, because they certainly aren't going to change their priorities, and I'm certainly not going to change my heart. These people peddle flesh for a living, so they really don't have to deal with what's really going on. What's really going on is that we are in a high-risk category and there is *still* very little condom use and no laws. I mean, the guys that work in the manufacturing and distribution warehouses that pack the boxes all are required to have a Hepatitis B shot! And we aren't. We have nothing. The need for self-regulation in this industry is a must.

I'm not sure if I was asked to leave or resigned the Free Speech Coalition Board of Directors. In one afternoon, I know that I refunded their money and started the lease under AIM Health Care's name.

ANA: *Right down the street from Jim South's office…*

MITCH: Right. It was a good place to set up shop because people were going in and out of World Modeling, and we were able to grab them and pull 'em in and give them testing. Now, we're getting a track record. AIM Health Care is in its second year. We have a great facility and state-of-the-art testing, but it's a critical time because we're being looked at in terms of grant-funding, which I'm always petitioning for. At this time, the L.A. County Board of Health is extraordinarily pleased and is officially coming to visit us next week for evaluations in grant funding from the National Institute of Health and the Center for Disease Control in Atlanta. They're talking about national federal funding for what we do here. That's a big fucking deal! That's a mark of change for this business at the millennium.

ANA: *Why do you think the sex industry was so successful in staving off an epidemic?*

MITCH: I think that *[the business]* wasn't as transient as it is now. Back then there were the same 300 people working over and over again, over a 10-year block. And we were very social. We traveled in the same packs, we slept together, we fucked together, we went shopping together, we raised our kids together. It was a very small, close-knit group.

Then, of course, came the "mainstreaming of pornography." Once Magic Johnson got HIV, everyone knew someone with HIV and they became aware of it and we saw the stats change from gay men to families and teenagers and heterosexuals. Then we in the Industry went a little crazy, and with the onslaught of videotape, technology, and the Internet, the market got so flooded that a lot more transient people came in. And the newer, the better, you know what I mean?

ANA: *Fresh meat.*

MITCH: Exactly. And you have the exploitation factor, too. By that I don't mean what people do on camera, but the duplication factor. The actors are only paid once for doing a high-risk job. They don't get royalties. They don't get residuals. And their films are duplicated countless times and gross all this money that the talent never sees. But we are talking about real health risks here. We're talking about real people. This is not just a product that we are making. It's not the phone company; it's people who are having high-risk sex in front of the camera and getting paid *once* for it.

ANA: *I heard you've directed a few gay and bisexual videos.*

MITCH: Yeah, I've directed some gay, some bisexual, some dance films, S&M films. In a way, the gay market had been incredibly ahead because it had a tremendous amount of its talent pool wiped out in the early 80s. All from AIDS. So they started using condoms very early on, much earlier than the straight porn industry. I think there's a stigma attached to gay porn. I think it has to do more with homophobia than fear of HIV. Like certain girls won't work with a guy if they know they've worked with a gay male. It's very, very odd. But it's not just because of the high-risk category, but because most talent doesn't want to even be associated with gay porn or anyone that works in it.

ANA: *Are people getting over that? Or is it still a problem?*

MITCH: In a way people are. And they kind of have to. Truth is, everyone does everything. A lot of the guys were particularly afraid of it—but we found out later why. It's because they did a lot of transsexual work years ago that they didn't want people to see. Or maybe they needed some dough and did a masturbation scene for a men's magazine or something. And they were kind of ashamed that they compromised themselves that way and didn't feel comfortable with that. So, there were a lot of things that we were able to uncover and discover and discard from that homophobic nature. But gay and straight are two completely different worlds. It hasn't crossed over that well or that much.

We do serve a large gay clientele, primarily for HIV and drug & alcohol counseling. They don't come for testing.

ANA: *They don't?*

MITCH: No, the gay industry doesn't do testing because a lot of the performers are already HIV positive.

ANA: *That doesn't make any sense.*

MITCH: That's what they do. They use two condoms when they work HIV positive. Really, a lot of them are on HIV cocktails or protease inhibitors, and their viral load goes down low. This means their transmission level goes down as well. It's not healthy, it's not advised, but it's a fact. And a lot of the girls actually like to work with gay guys because it's that fantasy of turning the gay guy around, that sort of thing. So the girls bring in the gay guys for testing, and if they're negative they go ahead and work in adult films in the straight side. The straight side doesn't want people to work positive when there's penetration. They just don't. They'd rather do different masturbation things or low-risk things or even being in an instructional video about being positive and so on. It's just a little different.

ANA: *What's the standard level of knowledge that new, younger people who want to be in adult films bring to you?*

MITCH: Well, the standard knowledge level is: there are no stupid questions. The level is about 5th or 6th grade. And that's in terms of everything: reading comprehension, understanding the issues and even basic sex education: "Where does the egg come from and how does it attach itself to the wall of the uterus and how does the sperm fertilize the egg?" That sort of thing. Basic Sex 101 we need to go over, and Basic HIV 101 and Hepatitis 101. We also suggest diet regimens for people if they're working really heavily. We recommend *Immunoplex* and things like that. We also have free nutritional assessment as well as free workout and body assessments given by doctors who come in once a month to do it. There are certain things you need to have in your immune system because it's just being blasted over and over again. You really need to get a lot of sleep, work out and have a good balance of proteins, carbohydrates and fats.

It's not because the people aren't intelligent, it's the *denial*: "My god, not me! Because I'm going to be glamorous and show it off, but I really don't want to think of that." So prevention education is our primary work here. We don't want to motivate; I don't really want to get involved with 'To Condom or Not To Condom.' It's not that I don't care—but I choose not to say it because my funding comes from a variety of different companies in this Industry, some of which are condom-only, condom-optional, or non-condom. When I went to these different companies, it turned into a fuckin' war, so I had to be very careful about how political I was. And the non-condom companies test their people every two weeks, bring them in for special counseling on STD's, and the non-condom companies pay for it. A lot of condom companies don't even do *that*. It's very odd.

ANA: *There are some disreputable producers and filmmakers, though.*

MITCH: Oh yeah! Any asshole with a hard-on and a camera. I know it's hard. I know this industry reeks of desperate people. I know you need to pay the rent and feed the baby. I know, I really do know. When immediacy calls, there's pornography. And what AIM Health Care does is stand in between that desperate feeling and the 24 hours it takes to get the test back. We can inform them, but we can't motivate them. But we can provide them with enough education so they can make informed choices, which is what they weren't getting before. So we are clearly a major part of the solution when it comes to distributing information. We always tell our people to hold their standards and boundaries. The most successful ones come in with a plan. They are able to think, "Well, how am I going to like this Industry? Am I going to be able to work in a few magazines, do six or seven movies so far this year and then maybe go on the road dancing and maybe pump up that Internet site?" And conceivably, in three or four years you could be in the real estate business or investing it wherever you may.

ANA: *Does this apply to men, too?*

MITCH: Men are a little different. Men are a little shut down, although they are the strength of this industry. The women are the commodity, so they call the shots. Woodsmen are very interesting folk. Remember that there is a strange dynamic in pornography. It's very, very hard to do what we do for a living on a daily basis and have someone genuinely love you for what you do. Performing acts of intimacy without the intimacy leaves a very empty hole. No matter what you try to fill that hole with, whether it's more of anything, it'll never fill that hole. Human nature is that we need other people to be with the rest of our lives. In the adult film industry, the love comes from each other and working together. It's hard for men in this business. It's hard on the women, but women are more communicative by nature. Men are not.

ANA: *Do the male performers come here and express those things?*

MITCH: Private and alone, yes. I cannot get them into a support group. Women will come in for evening support groups, but men will not. It's very difficult for someone to be able to face that moment of rejection when they say, "Well, this is what I do for a living." If there's a partner who is not ready to hear that, they're going to take that as who you are, what you are. Clearly, it's not. I don't know if you've been on a set, but it is sheer, pure hard work. It's different positions in high heels that you need to be a fucking contortionist to perform. It's very hard to have intimacy in that situation. People just don't fall in love when they've got hot lights going up their ass. Clearly, the sex act has very little to do with why people are drawn to this line of work. They can make money immediately. It's instant gratification—not always a good thing. I mean, if you were to ask me ten years ago how I was, I could tell you when I was going on tour, what dress I was wearing, what limo I would be riding in... I could tell you everything I *had,* but I could tell you very little about what I *felt* or who I was. I could just get really high and do what you wanted me to do. That was the basis of my life. Not a bad thing, but kind of sad.

ANA: *There's a great line in* **Kamikaze Hearts** *where Tiger [Sharon's girlfriend and heroin partner at the time] tells you, "You are such a success, but yet you're such a failure; that's why I love you."*

MITCH: Wow, you remember that movie! That's about 15 years old. I wanted to document that. It was important for me to capture the throes of addiction and shooting up on camera and my life with her and the way it was. Even after viewing it, I felt good about the truth in that. I was never willing to be truthful about anything in any other area in any other time during that time period. I was honest just for that movie. And it didn't have any effect on me. I thought it was cool, actually, because at that point in my life I really thought I was just going to die soon anyway. I was going for the big fuckin' James Dean finale, whatever it was going to be.

But as the years went on, I wasn't dying. I sure tried. I tempted the universe in a lot of ways. I continued to be very unhappy. I mean, I tried to let people get close to me, but I had a big secret I couldn't divulge. Now try being a heroin addict and not telling the person you care about. With heroin, you leave a trail of emotional wreckage and affect the lives of a lot of people in a most negative way. But when you're sober you can affect the lives of thousands, millions of people. Now that I am sober, I'm glad there are 24 hours in the day, because there's just so much to do. I have a lot left to accomplish!

Appendix

A. TALENT AGENTS

World Modeling Talent Agency
4523 Van Nuys Boulevard, Suite 203
Sherman Oaks, CA 91403
Phone: (818) 986-4316; Fax: (818) 986-9487
www.worldmodeling.com
(Attention: Jim South)

Reb's Pretty Girl International
7494 Santa Monica Boulevard, 2nd Floor
West Hollywood, CA 90048
Phone: (323) 882-8262
www.prettygirl.com
(Attention: Reb Sawitz)

Beautiful Models International
11385 Expo Boulevard, Suite 150
Los Angeles, California 90064
Phone: (310) 207-4622; (818) 603-5942
www.better-business.com/bmifmod.htm
(Attention: Regan Senter)

CHN International
7428 Santa Monica Blvd.
Los Angeles, California 90046
Phone: (323) 874-8252
(Attention: Hal Guthu)
Bring your own pictures; they deal exclusively with models for still magazine pictorials.

B. SUPPORT ORGANIZATIONS

[As you will notice, a majority of these clubs have the same contact info. Bill Margold started or is involved with all of them.]

Fans of X-Rated Entertainment (F.O.X.E.)
8231 DeLongpre Ave., Suite 1
West Hollywood, California 90046
Phone: (323) 650-7121; Fax: (818) 501-7502
(Contact: Bill Margold)
Send name, address, phone number and $25 for 1-year membership.

Free Speech Coalition (F.S.C.)
8231 DeLongpre Ave. Suite 1
West Hollywood, California 90046
Phone: (323) 650-7121; Fax: (818) 501-7502
http://www.freespeechcoalition.com
The X-rated industry's political action committee.

Protecting Adult Welfare (P.A.W.)
4523 Van Nuys Boulevard, Suite 205
Sherman Oaks, CA 91403
HelpLine: (800) 506-4999
Office: (818) 501-6139; Fax: (818) 501-7502
(Contact: Bill Margold)
Peer counseling and advising for adult performers.

C. INDUSTRY EVENTS

Adultex (Adult Entertainment Expo)
For more info, contact Tradeshow Productions:
Phone: (765) 651-9872; Fax:: (765) 651-1223
www.adultex.com

AVN Adult Entertainment Expo
(Concurrent with the Video Software Dealers' Association)
Phone: (213) 741-1151; Information: (818) 461-0980
www.vsda.org

Consumer Electronics Show (C.E.S.)
Check www.cesweb.org for updates.

East Coast Video Show
National: (800) 331-5706; Information: (714) 513-8682
www.ecvshow.com

Erotica L.A.
Phone: (818) 734-9898; Fax: (818) 888-9560
www.erotica-la.com
Adult marketplace and entertainment extravaganza.

Exotic Dancer Convention
Information: (727) 726-3592
www.exotic-dancer.com

Exotic Dancer Fan Fair
Information: (727) 726-3592
www.exotic-dancer.com
Over 150 of the industry's top feature performers, centerfolds, and porn
stars.

Interactive 2000 (I.A. 2000)
General information: (818) 786-4286; Fax: (818) 786-4347
www.ia2000.com
Over 100 exhibitors from the adult internet and audiotext industry.

AVN Awards
National: (800) 521-2474; Local: (818) 786-4286; Fax: (818) 786-0443
http://www.avn.com/awards/menu.html
The biggest adult awards show of the year, with over 90 categories.

F.O.X.E. Awards
January; Sunday before President's Day
Only members or performers are admitted.
Contact Bill Margold at (323) 656-6545

Night of the Stars
Sponsored by the Free Speech Coalition
Phone: (818) 348-9373; National: (800) 845-8503

The Coldwater Cats
(Bill Margold's pick-up touch football games)
Every Saturday, rain or shine.
Rancho Park, at Pico Blvd. & Motor Ave., Los Angeles, California
Noon-3pm (Game is at the field near the field house; look for Bill
Margold wearing his snazzy red sweat pants.)

Curveball
Late August on Blair Field
4700 Deukmejian Dr., Long Beach, CA 90804

Phone: (714) 703-4553; Sponsor & Talent Information: (714) 748-3526
www.curveball99.com
An all-porn star softball game to benefit Self-Awareness for Disabled
Americans.

D. HEALTH/MEDICAL SERVICES

Adult Industry Medical Health Care Foundation (AIM)
14241 Ventura Boulevard, Suite 105
(1½ blocks east of Van Nuys Blvd., 5 doors west of the Guitar Center)
Sherman Oaks, CA 91423
Phone: (818) 981-5681; Fax: (818) 981-3851
www.aim-med.org
Hours: 10am-5:30pm Mon-Fri; 1-5pm Sat.
(last blood draw for next day's results 4pm)

North Hollywood 10-Minute HIV Test Center
12910 Victory Boulevard
North Hollywood, CA 91601
Phone: (818) 760-4500

Planned Parenthood
(Branches in Burbank, Canoga Park, East L.A., Hollywood, Lawndale,
Pomona, Van Nuys and Whittier)
For exact locations call (323) 226-0800 or (818) 843-2009

AIDS Clinic for Women
3860 W. Martin Luther King Jr. Blvd., Crenshaw, CA
(323) 295-6571

AIDS Project Los Angeles
1313 N. Vine St., Hollywood, CA
Phone: (323) 993-1600
24-hour hotline: (800) 922-2437; Multilingual hotline: (800) 922-2438

Jeffery Goodman Special Care Clinic
1625 Schrader Blvd., Hollywood, CA
(323) 993-7500

L.A. Free Clinic
8084 Beverly Blvd., West Hollywood (323) 653-1990
6043 Hollywood Blvd. (213) 462-4158.

Hollywood-Sunset Free Clinic
3324 Sunset Blvd., Hollywood, CA
(323) 660-5715

Family Planning Associate Medical Group
12304 Santa Monica Blvd., Santa Monica, CA
(310) 820-8084

Southern California HIV/AIDS Hotline (800) 590-2437
LA County Department of Mental Health (800) 854-7771
LA Suicide Prevention Hotline (213) 381-5111
Pregnancy Hotline (800) 743-7348
CDC National HIV & AIDS Hotline (800) 342-2437
Alcoholic's Anonymous (323) 936-4343
Narcotics Anonymous (800) 248-6299
Cocaine Anonymous (800) 262-2463
Marijuana Anonymous (800) 766-6779
Gambler's Anonymous (888) 297-6191
Eating Disorders (818) 766-5663
Adult Children of Alcoholics (818) 342-9863
LA Commission on Assaults Against Women Rape Hotline
(213) 626 3393 [central L.A.] (310) 392-8381 [L.A. County]
National Domestic Violence Hotline (800) 779-3512
Rape Crisis Hotline (310) 392-8381

E. PRODUCERS OF ADULT CONTENT

ADAM AND EVE
302 Meadowland Dr., Hillsborough, NC 27278
Phone: (919) 644-8100; Fax: (919) 644-8150
www.adamandeve.com
Videos, books, novelties

ADAM FILM WORLD
8060 Melrose Avenue, Los Angeles, CA 90046
Phone: (323) 653-8060
www.adamfilmworld.com
Magazines

ADULT STARS MAGAZINE
1008 West Hallandale Beach Blvd., Hallandale, FL 33009
Phone: (954) 458-0021; Fax: (954) 454-7009
www.adultstarsmagazine.com
Books and magazines

ALL GOOD VIDEO
18034 Ventura Blvd., #491, Encino, CA, 91316
Phone: (818) 780-2229; Fax: (818) 989-2229
www.allgoodvideo.com
Videos

ALL WORLDS VIDEO
3487 Kurtz Street, San Diego, CA 92110
Phone: (619) 523-9500; Fax: (619) 225-6215
www.allworldsvideo.com

ANABOLIC VIDEO
534 Victoria Ave. #3; Venice, CA 90291
Phone: (310) 827-9088; Fax: (310) 822-7173
www.anabolic.com
Videos

ASTRAL OCEAN CINEMA / JILL KELLY ENTERTAINMENT
9510 Vassar Ave., Chatsworth, CA 91311
Phone: (800) 839-8279; Fax: (818) 886-0017
www.astralocean.com
Videos, CD-ROM, DVD

AVE ENTERTAINMENT
310 Townsend Street, #428, San Francisco, CA 94107
Phone: (415) 882-8394; Fax: (415) 882-7329
www.avexx4x.com
Videos, DVD, CD-ROM

THE AVI GROUP
P.O. Box 91257, Los Angeles, CA 90009
Phone: (802) 222-9622; Fax: (310) 574-2329
www.avigroup.com
Videos

AVN PUBLICATIONS. INC.
6700 Valjean Ave., Van Nuys, CA 91406
Phone: (818) 786-4286; Fax: (818) 786-4287
www.avn.com
Books and magazines

BIG TOP VIDEO
214 West Giant Road, Tucson, AZ 85705
Phone: (800) 342-3399; Fax: (520) 670-1422
DVD, Videos

BIZARRE VIDEO
20-40 Jay Street, Brooklyn, NY 11201
Phone: (718) 802-1251; Fax: (718) 802-0463
Specialty and Fetish Videos

BRUSH CREEK MEDIA
2215-R Market #148, San Francisco, CA 94114
Phone: (800) 234-3877; Fax: (415) 552-3244
www.brushcreek.com
Books and magazines, DVD, Videos

CANDID CAM ENTERTAINMENT NETWORK. INC.
111 Travelers Way N., St. Petersburg, FL 33710
Phone: (727) 347-8437; Fax: (727) 347-9427
www.candidcamproductions.com
Amateur videos

DAVE CUMMINGS PRODS.
4130 La Jolla Drive, Suite 107-92, La Jolla, CA 92037
www.davecummings.com
Videos

DIGITAL PLAYGROUND INC.
16134 Hart Street, Van Nuys, CA 91406
Phone: (818) 376-8488; Fax: (818) 376-8489
www.digitalplayground.com
CD-ROM, DVD, Videos

DIGITAL SIN
21345 Lassen Street, Suite 400, Chatsworth, CA 91321
Phone: (818) 773-4999; Fax: (818) 773-8020
www.newsensations.com
DVD

EAST WEST PRODUCTIONS INTERNATIONAL
P.O. Box 1398, Providence, RI 02901
Phone: (401) 453-5306; Fax: (401) 421-9480
www.lifestyle.com/swingers
Books and magazines

EDEN RAE ENTERTAINMENT
PO Box 2732, Hollywood, CA 90078
Phone: (888) 699-2705
Videos

EGAMII GROUP INCORPORATED
5225 Canyon Crest Drive, Suite 71-347, Riverside, CA 92507
Phone: (909) 721-0077; Fax: (909) 342-0025
www.egamii.com
Videos, Internet Video Solutions

ELEGANT ANGEL VIDEO
9801 Variel Ave., Chatsworth, CA 91311
Phone: (818) 773-0411; Fax: (818) 773-1163
Videos

ELDORADO
1840 Commerce, Boulder, CO 80301
Phone: (800) 525-0848; Fax: (303) 444-4622
Apparel, Books and magazines, Novelty Products, Videos

EVIL ANGEL VIDEO
14141 Covello Street, #8C, Van Nuys, CA 91405
Phone: (818) 787-1414; Fax: (818) 902-1414
www.buttman.com, www.buttmanmagazine.com
Magazines, DVD, Videos

EXTREME VIDEO ASSOCIATES
9428 Eton Ave., Unit K, Chatsworth, CA 91311
Phone: (818) 779-6479
Videos

FANTASY OUTLET
584 Castro, #134, San Francisco, CA 94114
Phone: (415) 376-3504
www.fantasyoutlet.com
CD-ROM, DVD, Videos, Star Signing

FILMWEST PRODS.
686 S. Arroyo Parkway, Suite 10, Pasadena, CA 91105
Phone: (818) 791-5800; Fax: (818) 791-5801
www.maxhardcore.com
Max Hardcore videos

HOMEGROWN VIDEO
P.O. Box 420820, San Diego, CA 92142
Phone: (619) 541-0280; Fax: (818) 541-0210
www.homegrownvideo.com
Amateur videos; will buy submittals.

INTERNET ENTERTAINMENT GROUP
2025 First Ave., Suite 1050, Seattle, WA 98121
Phone: (800) 882-9215; Fax: (206) 622-3706
www.ientertain.com
Videos, Internet content

INFLUX VIDEO
1671 W. Grant Rd., Tucson, AZ 85745
Phone: (888) 291-2987; Fax: (520) 623-9303
www.influxvideo.com
DVD, Internet web sites and services

L.B.O. ENTERTAINMENT
7959 Deering Avenue, Canoga Park, CA 91304
Phone: (800) 695-6909; Fax: (818) 598-6721
Fetish Videos

L.F.P., INC.
8484 Wilshire Blvd., Suite 900, Beverly Hills, CA 90211
Phone: (323) 651-5400
www.hustler.com
Magazines

LYONS VIDEO
21414 Chase Street, #1, Canoga Park, CA 91304
Phone: (818) 885-8738; Fax: (818) 885-0783
Videos

METRO, INC.
16557 Arminta Street, Van Nuys, CA 91406
Phone: (818) 988-1067; Fax: (818) 988-3948
www.metroglobal.com
DVD, Videos

MIDNIGHT FILM & VIDEO / EROTIC ANGEL PICTURES
9057 Eton, Chatsworth, CA 91311
Phone: (818) 772-4201; Fax: (818) 772-4245
www.midvid.com
CD-ROM, DVD, Videos

NEW BEGINNINGS. LTD.
11537 Bradley Ave., San Fernando, CA 91340
Phone: (800) 722-8797; Fax: (818) 361-0733
www.newbeginningsltd.com
Books and magazines, CD-ROM, DVD, Novelty Products, Videos

NEW SENSATIONS
21345 Lassen Street, Ste. 100, Chatsworth, CA 91311
Phone: (818) 773-4999; Fax: (818) 773-8020
newsensations.com
DVD, Videos, Other

OGV/PRIVATE
8599 Venice Blvd., #C, Los Angeles, CA 90034
Phone: (800) 397-5114; Fax: (310) 202-0897
CD-ROM, DVD, Videos

PASSION PICTURES
18215 Burbank Blvd., Suite 7, Tarzana, CA 91356
Phone: (818) 757-0007; Fax: (818) 774-0456
kissesatnight.com; hollywoodpornstars.com
DVD, Videos, CD's

PORNICATION
P.O. Box 71744, Madison Heights, MI 48071
Phone: (888) 844-9810; Fax: (248) 528-3889
www.pornication.com
Adult Internet Services, i.e. live models

PURITAN VIDEO PRODUCTIONS
1146 N. Irving Street, Allentown, PA 18103
Phone: (610) 433-2116; Fax: (610) 433-5895
www.puritaninternational.com
Books and magazines, DVD, Videos

RAVEN HILL STUDIOS
2280 5th Avenue South, St. Petersburg, FL 33712
Phone: (727) 327-4680; Fax: (727) 323-2935
wwwv.ravenhillstudios.com
Videos, CO-ROMs, Books and magazines, Novelty Products

REDBOARD VIDEO & ALLAN ALAN PICTURES
P.O. Box 2069, San Francisco, CA 94126
Phone: (415) 243-9606; Fax: (415) 243-9611
www.redboard.com; www.newmeat.com
Videos

S.A.W.S.I BVP PRODUCTIONS
7535 White Oak, Reseda, CA 91335
Phone: (818) 343-0742 ; Fax: (818) 881-9627

www.webopp.com; www.bluevideo.com
Internet Websites and Services

SEDUCTION ENTERPRISES
16515 Arminta Street, Van Nuys, CA 91406
Phone: (818) 782-2268; Fax: (818) 782-2242
Videos

SINTHETIC VIDEO
92 Corporate Park, Ste. C275, Irvine, CA 92606
Phone: (949) 252-1010; Fax: (949) 252-8084
www.electricplanet.com
CD-ROM, DVD, Videos

SNATCH PRODUCTIONS / SAMURAI VIDEO
9610 De Soto Avenue, Chatsworth, CA 91311
Phone: (818) 734-1610; Fax: (818) 734-1616
www.snatch.com; www.samuraiwomen.com

SUNSHINE FILMS
(aka Factory Home Video)
7722 Densmore Ave., Van Nuys, CA 91406
Phone: (818) 901-6350; Fax: (818) 901-6358
DVD, Videos

TIP TOP ENTERTAINMENT USA
5460 N. Peck Road, #J, Arcadia, CA 91006
Phone: (626) 305-7276; Fax: (626) 305-7278
www.adulttiptop.com
DVD, Videos

VCA PICTURES
9650 De Soto Ave., Chatsworth, CA 91311
Phone: (800) 421-2386; Fax: (818) 718-8536
CD-ROM, DVD, Videos

VCX
13418 Wyandotte Street, N. Hollywood, CA 91605
Phone: (818) 764-1777; Fax: (818) 764-0231
www.vcx.com
Videos

VIDEO TEAM
15753 Stagg Street, Van Nuys, CA 91406
Phone: (818) 997-3311; Fax: (818) 997-3338

Videos

V.I.P. SERVICES
21521 Strathern Ave., Canoga Park, CA 91304
Phone: (818) 702-8700; Fax: (818) 702-9100
Videos, DVD, CD-ROM

VIVID VIDEO
15127 Califa Street, Van Nuys, CA 91411
Phone: (818) 908-0481; Fax: (818) 908-1526
www.vividvideo.com
DVD, Videos

WEBPOWER. INC.
3918 Via Poinciana, Lake Worth, FL 33407
Phone: (561) 963-8507; Fax: (561) 963-9007
www.amateurs.com
Internet content

WEST COAST PRODUCTIONS
8040 Remmet Ave., Suite 11, Canoga Park, CA 91304
Phone: (818) 595-1191; Fax: (818) 595-1194
www.westcoastprod.com
Videos

WICKED PICTURES
9040 Eton Ave., Canoga Park, CA 91304
Phone: (818) 349-3593; Fax: (818) 349-6620
www.wickedweb.com
DVD. Videos

WORLDWIDE MEDIA GROUP
162 East 64th Street, New York. NY 10021
Phone: (212) 688-3556; Fax: (212) 688-1217
www.peepshow.com
Internet content

ZANE ENTERTAINMENT
21526 Osborne Street, Canoga Park, CA 91304
Phone: (818) 772-9570; Fax: (818) 772-4454
www.zanevideo.com
CD-ROM, Videos, Brochures

F. DISTRIBUTORS OF ADULT CONTENT

A.D.I. DISTRIBUTORS
626-636 N. 5th Street, Philadelphia PA 19123
Phone: (800) 727-1713; Fax: (800) 229-0523
Apparel, Books and magazines,
CD-ROM, DVD, Novelty Products

CURTIS CIRCULATION
730 River Road, New Milford, NJ 07646
Phone: (201) 634-7447; Fax: (201)634-7495
Books and magazines, Store Fixtures

GENERAL VIDEO OF AMERICA
1945 Carroll Ave., San Francisco, CA 94124
Phone: (415) 468-5600
DVD, Novelty Products, Videos

IDEAL MEDIA MARKETING
111 West Main Street, Mesa, AZ 85201
Phone: (602) 649-9688; Fax: (602) 649-3242
Videos

INTERACTIVE DISTRIBUTION
7 Oak Place, Montclair, NJ 07042
Phone: (973) 783-3600; Fax: (973) 783-3686
www.newmachine.com
CD-ROM, DVD

INTERNET FULFILLMENT
8100 Remmet Ave., #1, Canoga Park, CA 91304
Phone: (818) 888-0055; Fax: (818) 888-2069
www.imfc.com
Internet Shopping

KNOB/RYDER ENTERTAINMENT GROUP
8610 Santa Susanna Place, West Hills, CA 91304
Phone: (818) 883-5662; Fax: (818) 888-0525
www.knobryder.com
DVD, Videos

KOMAR CO
3300 Clipper Mill Road, Baltimore, MD 21211
Phone: (410) 235-2200; Fax: (410) 235-1911
Books and magazines

LUCKY DISTRIBUTORS. INC.
4141 South Figueroa Street, Los Angeles. CA 90037
Phone: (800) 338-8439; Fax: (323) 232-4723
Books and magazines

MARINA PACIFIC DISTRIBUTORS
7077 Vineland Ave., N. Hollywood, CA 91605
Phone: (818) 503-7741; Fax: (818) 509-1435

PARADISE MARKETING SERVICES
1204 Avenida Chelsea, Vista, CA 92083
Phone: (800) 993-3664; Fax: (888) 810-3888

USX VIDEO DISTRIBUTION
7741 Alabama Ave., Unit 13, Canoga Park, CA 91304
Phone: (888) 757-0537; Fax: (818) 610-0331
www.usxvideo.com
CD-ROM, DVD, Videos

VICO DISTRIBUTORS
7044 Sophia Ave., Van Nuys, CA 91406
Phone: (818) 780-5474; Fax: (818) 780-5790

WILLIAMS TRADING CO.
1555 Route 73, Pennsauken, NJ 08110
Phone: (609) 662-3344; Fax: (609) 663-2059
www.williamstradingco.com
Apparel, Books and magazines, Novelty Products, Videos

G. STORES IN L.A. FOR LINGERIE AND SLUTWEAR

Agasi Fashion
2025 Eighth St., Downtown L.A.
(213) 483-6165

Cinderella Fashion
6711 Hollywood Blvd.
Phone: (323) 463-3525

Dream Dresser
8444 Santa Monica Blvd., West Hollywood
(323) 848-3480

Dynamite Boutique
6681 Hollywood Blvd.
(323) 463-7766

Frederick's of Hollywood
6608 Hollywood Blvd.
(323) 466-8506

Hollywood Wigs
6311 Hollywood Blvd.
(323) 466-6479

Mr. & Mrs. J
6620 ½ Hollywood Blvd.
(323) 463-1872

Retail Slut
7308 Melrose Ave., Melrose District
(323) 934-1339

Santa Discount
7910 Santa Monica Blvd., Hollywood
(323) 654-9222

Squaresville
1800 Vermont Ave., Silver Lake
(323) 669-8464

Trashy Lingerie
402 N. La Cienega Blvd., West Hollywood
(310) 652-4543

H. PORN TOYS & ACCESSORIES

The Pleasure Chest
7733 Santa Monica Blvd., Hollywood
(323) 650-1022

Le Sex Shoppe
6315 ½ Hollywood Blvd.
(323) 464-9435
(five other locations in L.A. County)

International Love Boutique
7046 Hollywood Blvd.
(323) 466-7046

Casanova's Adult World
7766 Santa Monica Blvd.
(323) 848-9244

Diamond Adult World
6406 Van Nuys Blvd., Van Nuys
(818) 997-3665

Drake's
7566 Melrose Ave., Melrose District (323) 651-5600
8932 Santa Monica Blvd., West Hollywood (310) 289-8932

Circus of Books
8230 Santa Monica Blvd., West Hollywood (323) 656-6533
4001 Sunset Blvd., Silver Lake (323) 666-1304

Magick & Fetish Shop
3934 Sunset Blvd., Silver Lake
(323) 660-1575

I. RECOMMENDED VIEWING

800 Fantasy Lane
The Adventures of Buttman
Alexandra
Amanda By Night
An American Buttman in London
The Anal Adventures of Max Hardcore
Baby Face
Barbara Broadcast
Behind the Green Door
Between Lovers
Black Orchid
Blackthroat
Bobby Sox
Buttman's Inferno
Buttman vs. Buttwoman
The 'Buttslammers' Series
The 'Buttwoman' Series
Café Flesh

Café Flesh 2
Candy Stripers
Catwalk, Parts 1 & 2
Chameleons
Charli
Conquest
Count The Ways
Curse of the Catwoman
Deep Throat
Desires Within Young Girls
The Devil in Miss Jones (DMJ)
DMJ3: A New Beginning
DMJ4: The Final Outrage
DMJ5: The Inferno
The Dinner Party
Directors' Wet Dreams
Dixie Ray, Hollywood Star
Dog Walker
Elements of Desire
The Erotic Adventures of Candy
Sean Michaels' 'Erotic City' series
The 'Extreme Sex' series
Erotika
Eruption
Every Woman Has A Fantasy
Face Dance
Anything from Candida Royalle's 'Femme' video line
Firestorm
Games Women Play
Hawaii
The Health Club
Her Name Was Lisa
Hidden Obsessions
House of Dreams
I Like To Watch
In Love
Insatiable
Insatiable II
Janine Extreme Close-Up (Pts. 1 & 2)
Jenna Loves Rocco
John Wayne Bobbitt Uncut
The Joy of Fooling Around
The Lady Is A Tramp
The Last Day
The Last X-Rated Movie

Latex
Les Femmes Erotique
Let's Get Physical
Little Girls Blue
Loose Ends
The Masseuse (Pts. 1 & 2)
Matinee Idol
Mr. Marcus's Neighborhood
New Wave Hookers 3
New Wave Hookers 4
Nightdreams
Night Trips
One Track Mind
The Opening of Misty Beethoven
Pandora's Mirror
Panty Raid
Persona
Pink Lagoon
The Pleasure Hunt
Pretty Peaches
The Private Afternoons of Pamela Mann
The Punishment of Anne
Raw Talent
The Red Garter
Roommates
Russian Roulette
A Scent of Heather
Secrets
Sensations
Seven Into Snowy
Sex & Sex 2
Sex World
The 'Shane's World' series
Scheherazade
Shock
Smoker
The 'Sodomania' Series
Squalor Motel
The 'Starbangers' series
Steamy Windows
Sunset and Divine
The 'Taboo' series
Talk Dirty To Me
Teenage Sex Kitten
Things Change: My First Time (Pts. 1 & 2)

Through The Looking Glass
Tiffany Minx
Torrid Without A Cause
Up 'n' Coming
The 'Venom' Series
V: The Hot One
The Voyeur
Wet Rainbow
Wild Goose Chase
World's Biggest Gang Bang 1 & 2 (D: John T. Bone)
Zazal

J. RECOMMENDED READING

Anderson, Paul Thomas. *Boogie Nights* (original screenplay). London: Faber & Faber, 1998.

Boston Women's Health Collective. *The New Our Bodies, Ourselves: A Book By and For Women.* New York & London: Touchstone/Simon & Schuster, 1992.

Butler, Jerry, with Robert Rimmer & Catherine Tavel. *Raw Talent: The Adult Film Industry As Seen By Its Most Popular Male Star.* New York: Prometheus Books, 1990.

Campbell, Kevin. *Video Sex.* New York: Amherst Media, 1994.

Dunn, Jancee. "The Rock-Porn Connection," *Rolling Stone, August 19, 1999.*

Ebner, Mark. "L.A. Confidential: The Disappearance of Viper, Porn Star" *Gear,* May/June 1999.

Faludi, Susan. "The Money Shot," *The New Yorker, October 30, 1995.*

Flint, David. *Babylon Blue: An Illustrated History of Adult Cinema.* London: Creation Books, 1999.

Ford, Luke. *The History of X: 100 Years of Sex in Film.* New York: Prometheus Books, 1998.

Gaffin, Harris. *Hollywood Blue: The Tinseltown Pornographers.* London: B.T. Batsford, Ltd., 1997.

Gardetta, Dave. "The Lust Tycoons," *Los Angeles*, December 1998.

Gettleman, Jeffrey. "L.A. Economy's Dirty Secret: Porn Is Thriving," *The Los Angeles Times*, September 1, 1999.

Johnson, Hilary. "How Triple-X Became One Big Zzzz..." *Buzz*, October 1995.

Konik, Michael. "Agent X," *Los Angeles*, April 1997.

Loria, Ana. *GET PAID FOR SEX! The Big Bad Book of Sex Opportunities For Men and Women*. Malibu: InfoNet Publications, 1999.

Margold, William, with Dutch Bishop & Stephanie Green. *The Porn Stud Handbook (All You Ever Wanted to Know about the X-Rated Industry but Were Afraid to Ask)*. Los Angeles: Bearly Decent Enterprises, 1999.

Mitchell, Sharon, and Nina Hartley. "Nina and Sharon Explain It All" (videotape) produced and directed by Nina Hartley and Sharon Mitchell, 60 min. (Free Speech Coalition, 1999).

O'Toole, Laurence. *Pornocopia*. London: Serpent's Tail, 1998.

Petkovich, Anthony. *The X Factory: Inside the American Hardcore Film Industry*. Manchester: Headpress, 1997.

Sager, Mike. "Little Girl Lost," *GQ*, November 1994.

Schlosser, Eric. "The Business of Porn," *U.S. News & World Report*, February 10, 1997.

Stein, Joel. "Porn Goes Mainstream," *Time*, September 7, 1998.

Stoller, Robert J., and I.S. Levine. *Coming Attractions: The Making of an X-Rated Video*. New Haven and London: Yale University Press, 1993.

Wilkinson, Peter. "Death of a Porn Queen," *Rolling Stone*, October 20, 1994.

Young, Toby. "The Maturbatrix," *Gear*, July/August 1999.

K. SAMPLE MODEL RELEASE FORM

For and in meaningful consideration of my engagement as a model by
_____, hereafter referred to as the photographer,
on terms or fee hereinafter stated, I hereby give the photographer, his
legal representatives and assigns, those for whom the photographer is acting, and those acting with his permission, or his employees, the right and
permission to copyright and/or use, reuse, and/or publish, and republish
photographic pictures or portraits or videotape footage of me, in which I
may be distorted in character, or form, in conjunction with my own or a
fictitious name, on reproductions thereof in color, or black and white,
made through any media by the photographer at his studio or elsewhere,
for any purpose whatsoever; including the use of any printed matter in
conjunction therewith. I hereby release, discharge and agree to save
harmless the photographer, his representatives, assigns, employees or any
person or persons, corporation or corporations, for whom he might be
acting, including any firm publishing and/or distributing the finished
product, in whole or in part, from and against any liability as a result of
any distortion, blurring, or alteration, optical illusion, or use in composite
form, either intentionally or otherwise, that may occur or be produced in
the taking, processing, or reproduction of the finished product, its publication or distribution of the same, even should the same subject me to
ridicule, scandal, reproach, scorn or indignity. I hereby waive my right to
inspect or approve the finished photograph, videotape footage or advertising copy or printed matter that may be used in conjunction therewith
or to the eventual use that it might be applied. I hereby warrant that I am
at least eighteen years of age, and competent to contract in my own name
in so far as the above is concerned. I am to be compensated as fol-
lows:_____. I have read the
foregoing release, authorization and agreement, before affixing my signature below, and I warrant that I fully understand all the contents thereof.

_____   _____

signature   date

_____   _____

name   address

_____   _____

witness's signature   address

L. GLOSSARY OF ADULT SEX INDUSTRY TERMS

ADR: Automated Dialogue Replacement. Technical term for "dubbing" or "looping" of voices on the soundtrack.

AFW: Adam Film World.

Amateur: Term referring to porn either produced or starring amateurs.

Auto-Fellatio: Performing oral sex on oneself.

AVN: Adult Video News.

Bestiality: Sexual intercourse with animals.

B&D: 'Bondage & Discipline.'

CBT: 'Cock and ball torture.'

Cheat: To move ones position or limb to accommodate the camera, as in "Cheat on your right leg a bit."

C-light: 'Cooze light.' A tiny light that illuminates the genital areas during difficult sex scenes. Many c-lights are mounted directly onto cameras.

Cowgirl: Woman on top, man lying on his back on the bottom.

C/P: 'Corporal punishment.'

DAP: 'Double-anal penetration.' Two cocks in one anus.

DeSade: Another term for sado-masochism (S&M).

Doggy-style: Sex with woman on all fours and the man behind her in the anus or vagina.

Dom: The 'dominant' male or female in a sex scene.

DP: 'Double-penetration.' One penis on the anus, one in the vagina.

DPP: 'Double-pussy penetration.' Two cocks in one pussy.

Down off the sticks: Term for using a handheld camera to film a sex scene.

D/T: 'Dominance training' or 'dirty talk.'

English: Whipping (crop, cane, etc.)

Facial: Semen ejaculated onto someone's face.

Feminization: Refers either to male cross-dressing or the tendency of porn to cater to women's fantasies (i.e., 'vanilla' or 'high-end').

Fisting: Technically, someone's entire fist in someone else's anus is considered legally "obscene" unless a thumb kept out of the anus is shown on-camera.

Fluffers: Girls who keep male performers aroused (a.k.a., 'fluffed' or 'tickled') between takes of a sex scene.

French: To orally stimulate the genitals.

Golden Shower: Urinating on someone. Also considered "obscene."

Gonzo: A style of taped or filmed porn that emphasizes the actors interacting with the viewer and the camera-as-participant in the onscreen sex.

Greek: Anal worship or penetration.

GS: Genital stretching (or 'genitorture').

G/S: Golden shower, or urination.

Hardcore: Explicit style of taped or filmed sex that shows onscreen genitalia, penetration and male orgasm.

HEVG: Hustler Erotic Video Guide.

High-end: Also know as "vanilla", "designer" or "couples" porn. Refers to classy, feature-length porn films, usually with around six sex scenes, designed for first-timers and couples (i.e., in 'high-end' porn, a 'gang-bang' is not a gang bang but an 'orgy,' and so forth). Some notable high-end directors include Paul Thomas, Michael Ninn, Andrew Blake, Candida Royale and Cameron Grant.

Kill fee: Some men will negotiate a minimum sum of money in case they agree to do a film and then can't achieve an erection. It guarantees at least they'll get paid something.

'The Linda Syndrome': A term coined by a journalist to describe ex-porn starlets who renounce their porn pasts in order to gain acceptance from the mainstream culture.

Loops: A filmed or videotaped sequence that shows sex acts out of context (i.e., no story or dialogue) and can be endlessly repeated.

Looping: The practice of editing a sex scene with the same footage in a continuous repeating cycle.

M & G Track: 'Moan and Groan' track. The dubbing of voices over a sex scene.

Missionary: The standard sexual position in a sex scene: man on top; woman on bottom.

Money Shot: The culmination of every sex scene is when the man has an ejaculation, hopefully onscreen. Also known as the "cum shot" or the "pop shot."

NT: Nipple torture or teasing.

Open: On-set term for making the talent aware of performing for the camera, as in "Open to the camera a little more."

PD: Psychodrama.

Pro: Prostitute; professional model.

Pro/Am: Euphemism for "professional amateur." Refers to amateur-style filmed or taped porn that uses professional actors and not first-time participants. Not considered real 'Amateur' porn.

Raincoater: Derrogatory sterotype of porn fan: dirty raincoat, no pants, hairy hands, pervertish nature—you know: you.

RCA: 'Reverse-cowgirl anal': woman on top; man on bottom.

RCDP: 'Reverse cowgirl double penetration': Woman in middle; one man on top in her pussy, one man on bottom in her anus.

Reverse Cowgirl: Vaginal sex with woman on top, facing away from the man.

Rim: Frenching the anal area.

Roman: Multiple partners, or orgies.

R/S: Rough stuff.

Sixty-nine: Oral sex with two performers lying head-to-toe.

Slutwear: Euphemism for clothes worn by porn starlets.

Softcore: A nonexplicit style of taped or filmed sex that does not show penetration or male erections or ejaculations. Softcore is the prime type of porn for the cable and hotel pay-per-view markets.

Spooning: Man and woman lying side by side, man behind the woman.

Squirting: Can refer to female urination, a female orgasm that is visible onscreen, or simply expelling water or any other fluid out of the vagina.

Stunt Dick (or Pussy): One performer's genitalia standing in for another's.

Sub: The 'submissive' male or female in a sex scene.

S&M: Sadomasochism.

Suitcase Pimps: Boyfriends or husbands of female performers who act as their "agents" or "business managers" without really doing much of anything for them.

Top: The dominant performer in a sex scene. In gay porn, the "top" is the one who does the penetrating.

TP: Triple penetration. Penises in mouth, anus and vagina.

TS: 'Transsexual.'

TV: 'Transvestite.'

Vanilla: Term, often used by those who make B&D or S&M films, referring to "straight" sex features.

V/A: 'Verbal abuse.'

W/S: Water sports (enemas, urination, etc.)

Waiting for wood: On-set term for the time spent waiting for male talent to achieve an erection for the camera.

Wall-to-waller: Low budget, one-day porn of the one camera, one bed, and a slice of pizza for lunch variety.

Woodsman: Term for the few, the proud, the brave of the male talent who can consistently get it up and cum on cue.

XD: 'Cross-dressing.'

M. LOS ANGELES FILM BOARD

Los Angeles County:
6922 Hollywood Blvd., Suite 606
Hollywood, CA   90028
Nationwide: (800) 201-5982
Local: (323) 957-1000
Fax: (323) 962-4966
Hours: 8am-6pm Mon-Fri.

Los Angeles City:
6922 Hollywood Blvd., Suite 602
Hollywood, CA   90028
Nationwide: (800) 201-5982
Local: (323) 957-1000
Fax: (323) 962-4966
Hours: 8am-6pm Mon-Fri.